W9-AMC-865

Spelling Simplified

Other Books by Judi Kesselman-Turkel and Franklynn Peterson

BOOKS IN THIS SERIES
The Grammar Crammer: How to Write Perfect Sentences
Note-Taking Made Easy
Research Shortcuts
Secrets to Writing Great Papers
Study Smarts: How to Learn More in Less Time
Test-Taking Strategies
The Vocabulary Builder: The Practically Painless Way to a Larger Vocabulary

OTHER COAUTHORED BOOKS FOR ADULTS
The Author's Handbook
The Do-It-Yourself Custom Van Book (with Dr. Frank Konishi)
Eat Anything Exercise Diet (with Dr. Frank Konishi)
Good Writing
Homeowner's Book of Lists
The Magazine Writer's Handbook

COAUTHORED BOOKS FOR CHILDREN
I Can Use Tools
Vans

BY JUDI KESSELMAN-TURKEL
Stopping Out: A Guide to Leaving College and Getting Back In

BY FRANKLYNN PETERSON
The Build-It-Yourself Furniture Catalog
Children's Toys You Can Build Yourself
Freedom from Fibromyalgia (with Nancy Selfridge, M. D.)
Handbook of Lawn Mower Repair
Handbook of Snowmobile Maintenance and Repair
How to Fix Damn Near Everything
How to Improve Damn Near Everything around Your Home

Spelling Simplified

**Judi Kesselman-Turkel
and Franklynn Peterson**

THE UNIVERSITY OF WISCONSIN PRESS

PLAINFIELD PUBLIC LIBRARY DISTRICT
705 N. Illinois Street
Plainfield, Illinois 60544

For Charles Rosenthal,
remembering all those evenings we memorized spelling lists

The University of Wisconsin Press
1930 Monroe Street
Madison, Wisconsin 53711

www.wisc.edu/wisconsinpress/

3 Henrietta Street
London WC2E 8LU, England

Copyright © 1983 Judi Kesselman-Turkel and
Franklynn Peterson
All rights reserved

5   4   3   2   1

Printed in the United States of America

Library of Congress Cataloging-in-Publication Data
Kesselman-Turkel, Judi.
Spelling simplified / Judi Kesselman-Turkel and Franklynn
Peterson.
   p. cm.
   Originally published: Chicago : Contemporary Books, c1983.
   Includes bibliographical references and index.
   ISBN 0-299-19174-5 (pbk. : alk. paper)
   1. English language—Orthography and spelling. I Peterson,
Franklynn. II. Title.
PE1143.K47   2003
428.1—dc21   2003045822

3 1907 00182 3326

CONTENTS

INTRODUCTION

Spelling Makes Sense

Once upon a time spelling was taught with rules and drills and students didn't get out of grade school until they could correctly spell most of the 1,500 or so words in most vocabularies.

But in the twentieth century, two changes took place. First of all, everyone's vocabulary increased tremendously through extended education and universal access to radio, TV, and the movies. At the same time, almost the entire educational establishment adopted the attitude that English spelling is a helter-skelter assortment of letters that have no relation to the sounds they spell, and that the ability to spell is a talent that can't be taught. In most schools, spelling ceased to be seriously and methodically taught. The result has been a generation or more of such poor spellers that even newspapers and books are full of misspelled words.

English is, of course, not completely regular. It's a changing language, and some of the changes in sound have not been accompanied by changes in spelling. But it's far more orderly than poor spellers have been led to believe.

Recent research has shown what good spellers have been able to figure out on their own: that spelling *does* make sense. For 85 percent or more of English words, spelling is so sensibly tied to a word's sound and meaning that all you need in order to spell correctly are (1) a good ear, (2) careful speech, and (3) an understanding of which letters stand for which sounds.* For much of our language, spelling generalizations can be made and then these rules can be applied to spell words that we're unsure of. There are even easy guidelines that tell us when to forget the rules and check with a dictionary.

This book is a complete spelling course based on those recent findings. It is only revolutionary because the findings have never been codified for adults before. As a course, it is not meant to be skimmed, but studied slowly, in short segments. Used this way, it will make good spellers of poor ones.

After using this book, feel free to write to us in care of our publisher. We love to get feedback and suggestions for future editions.

---

*For support of our statements, consult the Bibliography at the end of the book. We especially thank Elsie D. Smelt, Australian author of *Speak, Spell and Read English,* for her insights and organizational strategies in doing for her Australian readers what we hope to achieve for Americans; and we applaud the U.S. Office of Education for sponsoring the computerized spelling study (see Hanna, et al) from whose raw data we were able to support our own long-cherished hunches about the relative regularity of English spelling.

PART I
THE PATTERNS OF ENGLISH

1

How to Use This Book

Say the following words:

probably   recognize   nuclear

Did you say *recognize* or *reconize?* Did you say *probably* or *probly?* Did you say *nuclear* (which is correct) or *nucular* (the way even TV announcers are mispronouncing the word nowadays)?

If you say a word wrong, aloud or silently, you'll never learn to spell it correctly. That's why we ask you to do the following as you learn to spell the words in this book:

1. Look hard at every word written in heavy type.
2. Look away and sound out the word as you listen to it.
3. Write the word.
4. Proofread or check the word to make sure that you've written what you meant to write down.

So before you begin this book, find a pencil and paper (preferably a pad of paper, so that you can review your work as you go along) and keep both with the book until you're done. Also keep a dictionary nearby. Any kind will do, so long as it shows pronunciation.

Rules are best remembered if they're discovered instead of preached, so in many places we use exercises to help *you* uncover the rules. We urge you to work diligently at these exercises.

Spelling is best learned in short segments of no more than 20 minutes at a time. We've divided the book's chapters into

3

brief sections and suggest that you cover no more than one section at a time, doing each exercise as you come to it. *Before you begin a written exercise, check back here to make sure that you follow the four points outlined above.*

You'll be doing a lot of out-loud sounding, so work in a quiet place where you won't feel silly making odd sounds. English is partly irregular, despite the patterns we'll show you, so along the way we're going to ask you to memorize some words. We're sure you already know how to spell many of them. Memorize the remainder as you go along by tacking a daily list in the john or on the refrigerator, or take it along on the bus or in the car pool. Don't let words pile up on you.

We're going to assume that you know elementary grammar—the meaning of *noun,* for instance. We'll also assume that your reading vocabulary is good. If you come across a term in the text that you don't understand, look it up in the dictionary or a grammar book (for example, our companion volume *The Grammar Crammer*) before you read further.

As an adult, you have some ingrained spelling habits that have to be relearned. No habit can be changed overnight. But if you *use* each new habit as we teach it, you'll find your spelling remarkably improved in just a few short months.

Once you've finished the book and taken a short breather, we suggest that you reread it, redoing the exercises. The second time through, you'll find all the rules and patterns falling easily into place, and you'll never again be a poor speller.

Are you ready to enter the ranks of good spellers? Then let's begin.

2

Check Your Hearing

There are all kinds of written language. Some languages, for example Chinese, translate *ideas* onto paper and the sounds of the words have nothing to do with the way the words look. But English writing puts the *sounds* of words onto paper. If you can hear those sounds accurately, you can spell most words. (Although some words are pronounced differently in different parts of the country, for spelling most words your regional accent will not get in the way.)

EXERCISE 1

Do the following for each word in this list:

1. Look hard at the word.
2. Look away and slowly say it aloud, listening to it.
3. Write it down as you hear yourself say it.
4. Proofread to check what you've written.

pot
wig
mud
hen
dab

What pattern does the above list of words follow? Complete this sentence to show the pattern for writing sounds:

Each sound _____.

Did you write something like this: *"Each sound is repre-*

sented by one letter.''? If not, do it now. Later we'll modify this rule, but it's a good one to start with.

EXERCISE 2

Here's a list of words that will check how well you hear each sound in a word.

1. Read each word.
2. Look away and say it, listening.
3. Write it down.
4. Proofread your list against ours.

pin	flit	rift	strut	strap	wing
pen	pram	hump	blank	fifth	clothing
apt	grog	yelp	plump	chump	when
fro	slop	shaft	frond	cleft	which

A good speller can spell words even when he doesn't know their meaning. If you had trouble spelling any of the words in this list, you need to practice hearing regular consonant and vowel sounds. (List any misspelled words in the space provided at the end of this chapter.) If you had no trouble, skip to the Chapter Summary and then go on to Chapter 3.

Hearing practice

The name of a letter is not the same as its sound (except sometimes in the case of the vowels). For instance, the letter *t* is named *tee* and the letter *h* is named *aitch*. To learn how to spell quickly and accurately, you must forget the names of the letters and remember just their sounds.

Regular single consonant sounds

The following list includes all the consonant sounds that

are most commonly represented by a single consonant letter. (Chapter 9 will concentrate on double-letter consonants.) The names of most of these letters include the sound. *C, g, h, w,* and *y* don't, so pay careful attention to their sounds.

Some of the sounds listed below can be spelled in other ways, too. For now just learn these most common ways of spelling the sounds.

sound	*usual spelling*	*words that use the sound*
b	*b*	**bad, big, gibbon, emblem, combine**
c	*c*	**comet, clip, incur, uncap, antic**
d	*d*	**dab, band, folded, cardinal, drive**
f	*f*	**fan, fist, after, if, sift, unflap**
g	*g*	**get, grind, chagrin, angry, meager**
h	*h*	**hold, his, ahead, unhelpful, inhumane**
j	*j*	**joy, jay, unjust, disjuncture, project**
l	*l*	**lime, link, relate, careful, amiable**
m	*m*	**meet, aluminum, amuse, team, emblem**
n	*n*	**next, nose, win, tournament, candid**
p	*p*	**part, please, carp, desperate, compare**
r	*r*	**rug, far, argument, person, irk**
s	*s*	**say, simple, ask, musty, pass**
t	*t*	**tag, told, wit, tutor, astute**
v	*v*	**vote, wave, vivid, pervade, vivify**
w	*w*	**wit, wasp, renew, allow, aware**
y	*y*	**yen, yankee, yippee, coyote**

Notice that the consonant letters *k, q* and *z* are missing above. The *k* sound is the same as the *c* sound. It is written with a *c* almost 75 percent of the time, and most of the rest of the time it's written *ck*. (For a full discussion, see Chapter 10.) The letter *q* is not represented by a sound in English (see Chapter 13). The sound *z* is most often represented by the letter *s* and will be discussed fully in Chapter 8.

EXERCISE 3

Say aloud each sound listed above (for example, make a hissing sound for *s*), and then say each word that contains the sound, listening for the sound as you say it. Exaggerate each sound in the word (for instance, for *bad* say the *b* sound, then the *a* sound, then the *d* sound). Get into the habit of exaggerating until your ear is so well trained that you can hear the individual sounds without separating them.

EXERCISE 4

When you've gone through the list once, do it a second time. This time, (1) listen for the other sounds in the listed words; then (2) say other words that have each highlighted sound in them.

EXERCISE 5

If you still have trouble hearing a particular sound, open a dictionary to the words that begin with that sound, and sound out the words, listening carefully to the way they start. (Warning: Some words that begin with *c, g, p, s,* and *t* start with other sounds. For almost every sound you'll find a few exceptions. Don't let it throw you. Learning the regularities of spelling won't make you a perfect speller, only a very good one.)

Regular consonant cluster sounds

There are more consonant sounds in English than there are letters to represent them. To make up for this deficiency, we've adopted the practice of combining two (and sometimes three) consonants to represent the sound. When we hear one of these sounds, we have to remember to write not one letter but the combination of letters that represents it.

sound	usual spelling	words that use the sound
ch	ch, tch	child, witch, catch, rich, achieve
sh	sh	ship, cash, ashes, enshrine, mushy
th (soft)	th	thick, cloth, truth, enthrall, gothic
th (hard)	th	then, with, other, clothing, mother
hw	wh	when, whisper, whisk, awhile, whirl
ng	ng	wing, song, lung, bringing, dunking

We will look more closely at each of these consonant cluster sounds later on. At this time we just want to make sure that you can hear each unique sound.

Many people confuse the *ch* sound with the *sh* sound. *Ch* is a much stronger sound. To make it, imitate the chug-chug-chug of an old steam train. After you do that several times, go back and say the words we've provided for the sound, exaggerating the *ch*. *Sh* is a whisper. To make it correctly, say the "be quiet" sound several times: *sh, sh, sh.* Then say the *sh* words above. Make sure that you can hear the difference between the two sounds before you go any further.

The hard *th* sound and the soft *th* sound give people pronunciation trouble. Say the *th* in *thick* several times, and then do the same for the *th* in *then.* Do you notice that for the first *th,* the "soft" sound, you blow air between teeth and tongue but produce no sound—and that when saying the "hard" *th* you do make a sound? (Some linguists call them "unvoiced" and "voiced" for that reason.)

Many people incorrectly pronounce the word *with* with a soft *th* instead of a hard one, but this causes few spelling problems since both sounds are spelled the same. However, some people say *wit* or *wid* for *with,* and change *th* into *d* or *t* in other words as well. If you do, you're in spelling trouble. You need to conform your pronunciation more nearly to what's considered Standard American—at least when it comes to thinking about how to spell a particular word.

EXERCISE 6

Repeat the following words several times, carefully pronouncing each sound correctly. (Be sure to include the *d* sound in *width.*)

with   width

Are you pronouncing *with* with a hard *th* sound and *width* with a soft *th* sound? Can you hear the difference?

The *hw* sound has almost disappeared in American English pronunciation. Most people nowadays make the same sound (*w*) when saying both *wet* and *when.* There are only two ways to learn when *wh* is the correct spelling: (1) exaggerate the difference between the two sounds, pronouncing *hw* every time you read a *wh* word so that you train your mind's ear to think *hw,* and (2) memorizing all the words that have *wh* in them. Since there aren't many, we've listed them all in Chapter 13.

Notice that the *ng* sound is not quite the same as *n* + *g.* To say the *g* in *ng,* you begin a *g* sound but it gets stopped in the back of your mouth before you push any air through the sound. Many people pronounce the sound incorrectly, pushing the air through (which is fine for spelling purposes, since those of you who do will remember to add the *g* when spelling). But in some parts of the United States, end-of-word *ng* is pronounced as if it were just *n:* drinkin', slummin'. If you can't hear the difference between *ng* and *n,* you must remember to write *ng* according to rules of grammar. We'll discuss *ng* in greater detail in Chapter 13, along with the other consonant cluster sounds.

EXERCISE 7

Repeat Exercises 3, 4, and 5 for the consonant cluster sounds listed above.

Regular long vowel sounds

The vowels are not as regular as the consonants. There are many more vowel sounds in English than vowels to represent them. Therefore, not only does each vowel do double duty, standing for what we call a "long" as well as a "short" sound, but there are also combinations of vowels that represent sounds. Here we'll just list the most regular English sounds and the single letters that most often represent them. Later on we'll discuss rules to guide you in choosing among other spellings.

Notice that the *long* vowel sound is also the name of the letter that represents it. Don't confuse the two, but keep the idea of a letter's sound separated from its name.

sound	usual spelling	spelling words that use the sound
a	*a*	**gate, caper, mayor, placate, inane**
e	*e, ee*	**evil, weed, indeed, see, equal**
i	*i, y*	**bite, idol, decide, finite, try***
o	*o*	**ode, focus, pole, duo, poking**
u	*u*	**use, usual, reduce, fusion, conclude****

Regular short vowel sounds

sound	usual spelling	words that use the sound
a	*a*	**fat, cast, matter, staff, uncanny**
e	*e*	**men, let, west, fret, splendid**
i	*i*	**pig, wit, crib, fist, visit**
o	*o*	**cot, plod, flog, fodder, crock**
u	*u*	**but, slug, rump, uncle, fungus**

---

*For a complete discussion of this use of *y* see Chapter 19.

**Notice that the sound is *yu*—like the letter name—in words like *fusion* and *use,* but *u* without the *y* sound in words like *reduce* and *conclude.* We'll discuss this further in Chapter 19.

In daily speech, we slur some sounds and weaken others to the point where we've lost some of the original pronunciations that told us how to spell. If you teach yourself to think *visit* and *fungus* instead of *vis-t* and *fung-s* when you're thinking about writing, you'll never spell these words incorrectly. Many of the so-called natural-born spellers among us have learned this trick of exaggerated enunciation.

EXERCISE 8

Repeat Exercises 3, 4, and 5 for the long and short vowel sounds.

EXERCISE 9

Say the following words with exaggerated pronunciation. (We've italicized the letters that trip most people up.) Once you've said them several times, ask someone to test your spelling of them. List all the misspelled words at the end of the chapter, in the space provided.

bulle*t*in	h*o*listic	elim*i*nate
emin*e*nt	*a*ccelerator	lique*f*y
en*e*my	devel*o*p	*a*ccommodate
err*o*neous	des*c*ribe	de*v*ice
de*v*ise	di*v*ide	di*s*ease
di*s*aster	diff*e*rence	hypocri*s*y
ecst*a*sy	defi*n*ite	inevi*t*able
furn*i*ture	med*i*cine	presi*d*ent
prim*i*tive	pris*o*ner	mini*a*ture
impromp*t*u	laborat*o*ry	interes*t*ed
mathem*a*tics	fiery	envir*o*nment
per*h*aps	per*f*orm	several
parl*i*ament	practica*l*ly	signific*a*nt
stren*g*th	temper*a*ment	temper*a*ture

If you come from a part of the country where short *e* or

short *u* is pronounced almost like short *i* (in other words, *pen* is pronounced *pin* or *just* is pronounced *jist*), learn to lengthen the short *e* or short *u* sound for spelling purposes. For example, for *pen* say *peh-ehn*.

EXERCISE 10

Here's a list of words for practice in saying the short *e* and short *u* sounds:

fetch	**gesture**	**fence**	**get**	**comment**
must	**undo**	**runt**	**adjust**	**smudge**

Chapter Summary

Each English letter or letter cluster stands for a special sound. The sounds are discussed in this chapter.

Words to Learn

List here all the words you misspelled in Exercises 2 and 9, as well as any others that you want to learn to spell.

3

Syllables and Stress

In addition to the individual sounds that combine to make words, there are two other clues to spelling: syllables and stress. It's important to understand both concepts in order to spell well.

Syllables

Words can be made up of anywhere from one to a dozen syllables. Each syllable must include one (and only one) vowel sound, but it may also contain anywhere from *no* consonant sounds to four or more of them.

In order to count how many syllables there are in a word, count how many distinct vowel sounds you hear.

EXERCISE 11

Tell how many syllables are in each word. (If a word has more than one syllable, don't worry about where to divide the syllables. We'll discuss that later.)

pug	candid	mitigate	triumvirate
slant	also	correction	qualification
fist	blossom	beautify	ceremonial
a	fragrant	quantity	curiosity

Did you guess that all the words in the first column are one syllable, all the words in the second column two syllables, all the words in the third column three syllables, *triumvirate* four syllables, and the last three words in that column five syllables? Then you don't need any more help with syllabification. If you didn't guess correctly, go over the following exercise several times, until your ear recognizes how words break up into syllables.

EXERCISE 12

Read each of the following words slowly, syllable by syllable, hitting your hand on your lap to mark each syllable as if you were beating a drum. (We've begun with some words that are very easy to syllabify.)

na-tive	**or-der-ly**
sig-nal	**sim-i-lar**
up-set	**mu-si-cal**
op-tic	**con-du-cive**
can-did	**beau-ti-fy**
al-so	**quan-ti-ty**
pug	**dy-na-mite**
slant	**dy-nam-ic**
quack	**bat-tle**
blos-som	**tri-um-vi-rate**
fra-grant	**qual-i-fi-ca-tion**
mit-i-gate	**cer-e-mo-ni-al**
cor-rec-tion	**cu-ri-os-i-ty**

Although experts agree on what a syllable is, they don't always agree on where to divide syllables. Most popular is this method:

Following a long vowel sound, a consonant is usually put with the next syllable (*cy-clone*). Following a short vowel sound, a consonant is usually put with that syllable (*civ-il*) unless the next syllable is accented (*ci-vil'-i-ty*). If two separate consonants occur one after the other, one usually goes with the previous syllable and the other with the next syllable after a short vowel sound, but after a long vowel sound they both go with the next syllable (*fra-grant*). Consonant clusters are always treated as one consonant (*wash-er*).

If you were following this method, you would write *cer-e-mo-ni-al* correctly. However, in speaking we glide the *r* sound between the *ce* and the next *e* and it's almost impossible to hear whether it belongs with the first or second syllable. You would divide *blos-som* and *cu-ri-os-i-ty* as shown, but in speaking most of us say *blo-ssom* and *cu-ri-o-si-ty*. If you need to divide syllables correctly in writing, consult your dictionary. To spell correctly, it's usually enough to be able to distinguish how many syllables a word contains and approximately where they divide.

Stress

In almost all English words having more than one syllable, we come down harder on one syllable than any of the others. In addition, many words have another syllable that's given a midway stress. Luckily, in order to spell correctly you need not be able to differentiate light stresses—only the strong ones, since some spelling generalizations depend on whether the syllable is stressed strongly or not. (Stress will be important only when we get to Latin- and Greek-derived words.)

EXERCISE 13

To test your ear for stress differentiation, go back to the list in Exercise 11 and, for each word in the list, put an accent mark (') after the last letter in the stressed syllable. Check your answers against those at the end of the book.

If you marked all the words correctly, you don't need any more help training your ear to hear stress. Turn to Chapter 4. If you got some of the stress marks in the wrong place, do the following exercises.

EXERCISE 14

Read the following list aloud, reading each stressed syllable very loudly and each unstressed syllable very softly. Do it over and over, reading more and more quickly and naturally, until you can hear the difference when you're using normal-sounding speech.

(1)	*(2)*
na'-tive	or'-der-ly
sig'-nal	sim'-i-lar
up-set'	mu'-si-cal
op'-tic	con-du'-cive
can'-did	beau'-ti-fy
al'-so	quan'-ti-ty
pug'	dy'-na-mite
slant'	dy-nam'-ic
quack'	bat'-tle
blos'-som	tri-um'-vi-rate
fra'-grant	qual-i-fi-ca'-tion
mit'-i-gate	cer-e-mo'-ni-al
cor-rec'-tion	cu-ri-os'-i-ty

EXERCISE 15

Practice repeating aloud each of the following pairs of words, listening for the difference in stress in each pair:

dynamite (dy'-na-mite)	dynamic (dy-nam'-ic)
method (meth'-od)	methodical (me-thod'-i-cal)
rigid (rig'-id)	rigidity (ri-gid'-i-ty)
telephone (tel'-e-phone)	telephonic (tel-e-phon'-ic)

(The spelling *ph* for *f* sounds, and all other irregular spellings, will be discussed as we go along. For now, don't worry about them. One thing at a time!)

EXERCISE 16

For extra practice in hearing stress, there's nothing like reading aloud sing-song poetry, for instance the verses of Edward Lear and John Greenleaf Whittier. Longfellow, too, is full of regular stress patterns that will help train your ear. To start you off, mark the stressed syllables in the following famous stanza by Henry Wadsworth Longfellow and compare your marks with our answer at the end of the book.

> Life is real! Life is earnest!
>   And the grave is not its goal;
> "Dust thou art, to dust returnest"
>   Was not spoken of the soul.

Chapter Summary

1. There are as many syllables in a word as there are distinct vowel sounds.
2. Syllables with a long vowel sound always divide after the vowel. Syllables with a short vowel sound usually divide after the next immediate consonant or consonant cluster.
3. Consonant clusters are always treated as one consonant.
4. In multisyllable words, one syllable is nearly always stressed more than the others.

Words to Learn

Have someone test you on the words highlighted in this chapter, and write your personal demons here.

4

Big Words Come from Little Ones

A group of researchers spent several years and lots of the public's money feeding spelling rules into a computer and then asking the computer to spell the 17,000 or so words that comprise most educated persons' vocabularies. The computer only spelled about 50 percent correctly, but it would have gotten at least 85 percent if only the researchers had been able to perfect a rule so that the computer could recognize the fact that, in English, most big words (especially words of three syllables and more) grow from little words. Since most people easily recognize the little words, once you know how to spell those little words you're practically home free.

There are two ways in which big words are made. See if you can find the two ways by studying the following lists.

(1)	(2)
overrun	kindest
citywide	becoming
framework	disobey
cannot	agreeable
handkerchief	carrying
nevertheless	courageous
nineteen	thousandths
withheld	changeable
grapefruit	publicly
forehead	misspell
whalebone	leafless
careworn	enrich

(1)	*(2)*
steersman	abreast
spearmint	profiteer
sharecropper	nonconfidential
choirmaster	disestablishment
gingerbread	submarginally
busyness	recommend

We hope you figured out the following pattern: *Big words are usually made by (1) combining little words or (2) adding beginnings or endings to little words.*

When you're combining little words, you have to make sure that you spell the right little words. For example, the first part of *whalebone* refers to a whale, not a wail. The word that has to do with limiting the right to copy is *copyright,* not copywrite. The word *forehead* means the front (fore) part of the head, and has no relationship with the word *for. Busyness* is quite a different word from *business.* (If you don't know the difference, use a dictionary.) To help you, we have highlighted some of these homonyms (words that sound alike but are spelled differently because they mean different things) throughout the book. They must be memorized along with their separate meanings. If you're not familiar with a homonym's meaning, the only accurate guide is a dictionary.

Did you notice, in the second list of words above *(2),* that several beginnings and endings can be strung onto one little word? That's one of the most popular patterns for forming words in our language.

English started out as a Germanic language, and most of its regular spelling patterns come from those long-ago roots. Almost all the one-syllable words with simple *a, e, i, o,* or *u* vowel spellings (instead of *ou, ea,* and such), and some regular two-syllable words as well, are native English and are derived from the same words as modern German. You can recognize native English words not only from their regular-vowel spellings, but also from the ideas these words stand for. In general, they are *all the words needed to express the simple thoughts and activities in which people took part before they became educated and industrialized:* words like *food, sky, Sunday, ax* and *pig.*

But English also has two other kinds of words in it:

1. Latin and Greek words have been coming in since the time of the Renaissance and now comprise at least half of the words in an educated person's vocabulary. They follow a regular, orderly pattern of spelling and add prefixes and suffixes to make bigger words. We'll look at them in Part IV.

2. Invasion words came in mostly between the tenth and fourteenth centuries, though they're still trickling in today. They came from Norman, Saxon, Dutch, German, and even Eskimo words (*igloo* is Eskimo). Most of these words don't fit into regular English spelling patterns. However, a great many of them follow the pattern of our Latin imports. They are mostly words of one and two syllables where vowel sounds are written with more than one letter (*bait, weapon, haunch*).

Let's focus now on the words in the first and oldest group, native English. You've already studied them in school from a grammatical point of view. Here we'll concentrate on spelling, not grammar.

Chapter Summary

1. Big words are usually made by (a) combining little words, or (b) adding beginnings or endings to little words.
2. Native English and Latin- and Greek-derived words generally follow regular patterns of spelling. Invasion words don't.
3. Homonyms must be memorized along with their separate meanings.

PART II

REGULARITIES IN NATIVE ENGLISH WORDS

5

Native English Word Endings

Native English word endings all follow essentially the same pattern of spelling. Once you learn it, many spelling mistakes disappear. These are the most common English word endings:

-en	-ful	-less	-ness
-ly	-th	-ing	-er
-est	-ish	-ed	-y

Let's begin our study of these endings with an exercise.

EXERCISE 17

In the following words, cross out the common English endings. Examine the rest of each word to find the pattern for adding these endings to words:

soulful	guileless	fondness
dearly	growth	curbing
wished	soloing	hollowness
candidly	seventh	lovely
follower	misty	fixedness

Complete this sentence to show the pattern you observed: Common native English endings are added to _____

_____ .

Here's the pattern you should have found, restated: *Pattern for adding common endings (other than the z or s sound): Add the ending to the complete word.* This rule should help you spell many words you've had trouble with until now.

Get to know the common English endings listed above, so that you can recognize them at the ends of words. Then you'll never again have trouble spelling words like *resolutely* and *hundredth*.

Problems with -ed

The ending *-ed* is pronounced *t* after *p, k, f, th* (soft), *s, sh,* and *ch,* because it's hard to say the sound *d* after these sounds. Try it yourself with the following words:

trapped	**picked**	**doffed**	**unearthed**
missed	**vanished**	**pitched**	**passed**

Despite the *t* pronunciation, only a few common verb endings are actually spelled *-t*. Memorize them as exceptions to the *-ed* rule. (Notice how we've grouped them for easier memorization.)

crept	**felt**	**dreamt**	**burnt**	**left**
kept	**dealt**	**meant**	**built**	
slept	**knelt**	**sent**		
wept		**spent**		
swept		**bent**		

After a *t* sound, *-ed* is pronounced short *e + d,* simply because the *d* sound gets swallowed after the *t* sound:

outwitted	**carpeted**	**created**

These words cause no spelling trouble. Just spell them the way they sound, remembering to include the entire smaller word in the large one.

The ending -*ful*

The sound *ful* is spelled *ful* practically every single time in the English language. There are only three exceptions:

1. *full* and words made up of *full* + another word (*fullback, full-length*)
2. the word *full* + an ending (*fuller, fullest, fullness, fully*—but not *willfulness*)
3. the ending -*fully,* made up of -*ful* + -*ly* (*respectfully*)

In all other cases the sound *ful* is spelled *ful*—even the word *fulsome,* which means *abundant.*

The ending -*al* + -*ly*

Some Latin-derived words add the native ending -*ly* after the Latin ending -*al*. They sometimes cause spelling problems. Memorize these demons.

finally	**typically**	**occasionally**
unusually	**universally**	**formally**
generally	**especially**	

But notice that these words don't contain -*al*:

publicly   **particularly**   **formerly**

The following word is in the midst of a spelling change, and both forms are considered correct:

frantically   **franticly**

Final *s* and *z* sounds to show plural

Native English words are often made plural by adding a *z*

or *s* sound at the end. It is always spelled *-s.*

Most English nouns show plural by adding *-s:*

> one **house**   several **houses**
> one **proof**   several **proofs**

Notice that *houses* ends in a hard *s* (*z*) sound and *proofs* ends in a soft *s* sound. But both are spelled the same. [Some very old nouns (*child, ox, woman,* and *man*) make other changes to show plural. But all except *women* are spelled exactly the way they sound.]

If the noun already ends in an "s" type of sound (*s, ss, ch, sh, x, z*), we make sure that people know we mean plural by adding the sound *ez,* spelled *-es:*

> one **grass**   several **grasses**
> one **box**   several **boxes**
> one **witch**   several **witches**
> one **buzz**   several **buzzes**

Your ear should be able to guide you in spelling these words correctly.

If the noun ends in a *v* sound, we also add *-es.*

> several **wolves**
> two **halves**

Notice that the singular of these words is sounded and spelled with an *f* sound while the plural changes to *v.* Again, if you pronounce these words correctly and listen to them carefully, you'll spell them correctly every time. (There's only one English word that has a *v* sound spelled *f: of.*)

If the singular noun ends in the sound *o,* there isn't any pattern for correct spelling of the plural because our spelling of these words has been changing.

one **potato**   several **potatoes**
one **pro**   several **pros**
one **ghetto**   several **ghettos** or **ghettoes**

Your best bet is to consult a dictionary for words ending in *o*.

If the singular noun ends in a long *e* sound, spelled *y,* the *y* is usually changed to *i* and -*es* is added:

one **city**   several **cities**

We'll have more to say about this *y-i* ending in Chapter 19.

In the third-person-singular form of the present tense, verbs also have a *z* sound ending:

I **claim**   he **claims**
I **go**   he **goes**
I **come**   he **comes**
I **pity**   he **pities**
I **bless**   he **blesses**
I **wish**   he **wishes**

Compare the above spellings with the spelling rules we observed for plural nouns. Do these words follow those rules? _____

Then here's a rule that will take the guesswork out of when a final *z* sound is spelled -*s* and when it's spelled -*es:*

Pattern for spelling the z or s sound at the end of a plural noun or a verb: For words having v, *long* e *spelled* y *or* i, *or* s-*like sounds before the last z sound, the z sound is spelled* -es. *Otherwise it is spelled* -s. *Nouns ending in* o *are made plural with either* -s *or* -es.

Words to memorize

The following are the only common one-syllable words

that end in a *z* sound that are spelled *z*, not *s:*

fez   quiz   adz   whiz

Other demons that trip people up are:

tries   replies   buys   wholly (whole + *-ly*)

(See Chapter 19 for discussion of the *i-y* substitution.)

In some cases we seem to drop an *e* or to double the final consonant when adding the common endings.

lover   blabber   trapped   created

You'll have no trouble with these words once you've read the next two chapters.

EXERCISE 18

Find the misspelled words and spell them correctly:

hundreth	copicat
clocking	manyfeathered
spilld	fullfill
stowes	untimely
granpa	housemade
reviews	hartfelt
lanlubber	ghostly
willful	wherupon
goosberry	hurtful
stoves	fulminate
fleebitten	hurridly
blessedness	accustomd
yourselfs	foremost
learning	achievd
instigates	therefore
everthing	accidently

Chapter Summary

1. The most common native English word endings (*-en, -ful, -less, -ness, -ly, -th, -ing, -er, -est, -ish, -ed,* and *-y*) are generally added to the entire little word. In a few cases, *-ed* is changed to *-t*.

2. Native English words often add a *z* or *s* sound at the end to show a plural noun or a third-person-singular present-tense verb. For words having *v*, long *e* spelled *y* or *i,* or *s*-like sounds before the last *z* sound, the *z* sound is spelled *-es*. Otherwise it is spelled *-s*. Nouns ending in *o* are made plural with either *-s* or *-es*.

3. Only one English word spells the *v* sound *f: of*.

Words to Learn

Have someone test your spelling of all the demons and other words listed in heavy type in this chapter, and add your misspelled words to the demons listed below. Also add any words you spelled wrong in Exercise 18.

women
ninth
potatoes

6

When to Double Consonants

Researchers tell us that the greatest cause of spelling error is uncertainty about what letters stand for what English sounds. We've dealt with that in the previous chapters. The second and third largest causes of spelling error, coming right after the big one, are (1) uncertainty about when to double a consonant, and (2) uncertainty about when to put in a "silent *e*." Since these are two of the most easily solved problems in spelling, we'll next show you how to keep yourself from making these two mistakes. We expect these solutions to improve your spelling so much that you'll have added incentive to tackle the rest of the book.

This chapter will cover doubled consonants, and Chapter 7 will tackle silent *e*.

Doubling in the middle of a word

EXERCISE 19

Compare the following sets of words and see if you can find a pattern for doubling consonants:

diner	dinner
coma	comma
planed	planned
baring	barring
later	latter
canes	cans
caner	canner
trim	trimmed
pal	pallid
red	reddish

Pattern: A consonant is doubled when _____
_____ .

Did you write something like *"A consonant is doubled when
it follows a short vowel sound and there's another syllable
after it."*? Good for you if you noticed that *cans* doesn't
double the consonant because no syllable follows it. You're
almost completely correct.

But now compare the first- and second-column words in
the next list:

lobber	lobster
trussed	trusty
strumming	strumpet
hubbub	hubcap

Why is the consonant doubled in the first list? Because it
comes after a _____ vowel sound. Why isn't it doubled in
the second list? _____ .
Did you guess that it has something to do with the presence
of other consonants?
Does this definition hold true for the following words?

stripling   sapling   trimly   wanly

Now take a look at these words:

diner	later
coma	tubeless
planer	basin

Why isn't the consonant doubled?   _____ .
Did you notice the long vowel sound in front of each
consonant?
What's different about the words below?

cobbler	affront
fiddled	aggregate
huddling	saffron
bedraggled	diffraction

Did you notice that the root-word ending *-le* is hidden in each word in column one, and that the words in column two are not native English words? In Chapter 13 we'll discover that the *le* sound actually begins with a vowel sound, and in part IV we'll see the pattern for doubling that's followed by Latin- and Greek-derived words like the ones in column two.

Adding together all our findings, we can come up with a rule to guide us in spelling all the native English words of one and two syllables, and all the words that are built by adding to these words:

Rule for Doubling Consonants: Words with a long vowel sound (LVS) before the consonant are written vowel-consonant-vowel (VCV). Words with a short vowel sound (SVS) before the consonant are written vowel-consonant-consonant-vowel (VCCV). (Here's an acronym suggested by Australian teacher-author Elsie D. Smelt that may help you remember: *LVS = VCV, SVS = VCCV.*)

When an ending beginning with a vowel is added to a word whose final syllable includes a short vowel sound, the final consonant is doubled, if necessary, to complete the VCCV pattern.

This rule also works for many Latin- and Greek-derived words (*committed, commitment, committee*); but we'll look more fully at those words in Part IV.

Exceptions

As we present each spelling generalization, we will list often-used words that are exceptions to the rule. As you will see, most exceptions are made for logical reasons.

The most common reason for violating the doubled-consonant pattern is to distinguish between two words that sound alike, or nearly alike. To help readers, the first typesetters decided to spell each homonym differently.

in—inn
horse—hoarse
but—butt

The following consonant sounds are usually doubled at the end of a one-syllable word if they come after a short vowel sound:

f *sound (unless spelled* **gh** *or* **lf***):* **cuff, staff, off, whiff, cliff.** (Only exception: **if**)

l *sound:* The common English words that end in *-ll* are one-syllable words like **call, till, spell, mall,** and similar words. (Only exceptions: **nil, pal**)

s *sound after* **a, e, i,** *or* **o**: **dress, pass, miss, loss.** (Exceptions: **gas, its, madras, this, yes, axis, bias, oasis, chaos**) After *u,* the *s* sound is rarely spelled with a double *s* at the end of a word: **bus, thus.** (Exceptions: **cuss, fuss, discuss, truss**)

z *sound spelled* **z**: **buzz, fizz.** (Exceptions: **quiz, whiz, fez, adz, topaz**) (See also Chapter 8.)

Learn the above patterns and have someone test your spelling of the exceptions. Add your misspelled words to the list at the end of this chapter. Also learn these other common words that are exceptions to the general rule:

add	**odd**	**egg**	**all**
apple	**purr**	**mitt**	**imagine**

EXERCISE 20

Check your understanding of the rule for doubling consonants by correctly spelling each misspelled word in the following list. (Answers are at the end of the book.)

mummy	saflower	coping	afix
stoped	magnate	straddle	warant
depressed	append	medling	diging
fusion	appron	downtrodden	untill
dissmis	corupt	tatoo	
oficial	attract	sheriff	
dental	fliver	boondoggle	

Chapter Summary

1. Words with a long vowel sound (LVS) before the consonant are written vowel-consonant-vowel (VCV). Words with a short vowel sound (SVS) before the consonant are written vowel-consonant-consonant-vowel (VCCV). (LVS = VCV, SVS = VCCV.)

2. The spelling *-le* is pronounced as if it begins with a vowel. A consonant before *-le* is usually doubled after a short vowel sound.

3. The following consonants are generally doubled after a short vowel sound at the end of a one-syllable word: *f, l, s* (except after *u*), *z*.

Words to Learn

Have someone test your spelling of all the words in heavy type in this chapter, and write down every misspelled word. Also write down every word missed in an exercise. At the end of each chapter there's space for putting down the demons you find this way, so that you can memorize them.

7

Helping *e*

Back in Chapter 2, we asked you to accept the spelling rule that each sound is written as a letter or a letter cluster. In Chapter 6, we saw that sometimes a letter is doubled—but discovered a good reason for the doubling: It helps readers know that what comes before the doubled letter is a short-vowel sound, not a long one. So let's modify the first spelling rule right now:

Pattern for spelling English words: Each sound is represented by a letter except when there's a reason for doing otherwise.

We've already discussed the pattern for writing a consonant as a doubled letter (SVS = VCCV, LVS = VCV). Now compare the words in each line below and see if you can find the reason for putting an extra *e* in some words:

can	cane	caning	canebreak
tub	tube	tuber	tubing
rip	ripe	ripen	ripest
don	drone	drones	droning
spin	spine	spinal	spineless

A comparison of the first column and the second column should enable you to complete the following sentence: The letter *e* is added at the end of a one-syllable word to show that the vowel sound _____.

But now notice what happens when common endings (*-est, -ing, -less, -en,* and such) are added to the word. In some cases, we drop the *e* of the second-column word that gives it a long vowel sound. Can you see why? _____

_____ .

Did you guess that this pattern is related to the pattern for doubling consonants that we learned in Chapter 4? Let's review the part of that pattern that applies: To show that the vowel before the consonant is an LVS, English uses the pattern vowel-consonant-vowel (LVS = VCV). We don't need to put in an *e* to show that we're spelling *spinal,* not *spinnal,* because the pattern VCV is already there. We do need to put it in to show that we're spelling spine (an LVS) and not spin (an SVS).

Pronounce the following words:

spin   spinless   spine   spineless

Notice that we need to put in the helping *e* in writing *spineless* or people will think we meant *spinless.*

Many words take on a silent *e* after long *e, o,* or *u* endings even without a final consonant. Here are some examples. We're sure you can find others.

true	**foe**	**free**
construe	**hoe**	**agree**

A number of words that end in two consonants and have a final *s* sound add a helping *e* (instead of the usual doubled *s*) after the final *s* sound. Our language's codifiers seemed to feel that something was needed to indicate that the word isn't a plural noun. Some words that follow this pattern of using silent *e* as an indicator are:

else   false   rinse

To find another common situation in which *e* is added as a clue to pronunciation, study the following words:

cog	**cage**	**cogent**	**cagily**
hug	**huge**	**hugely**	**hugeness**
rug	**oblige**	**obliging**	**argument**
lung	**lunge**	**lunging**	**lunged**
rang	**arrange**	**arranging**	**arrangement**

Why do you think we add an *e* to the words in column two? To show that the letter *g* _____.
(We'll discuss it again in Chapter 11.) Look at the rest of the words. When does adding a helping *e* make the vowel an LVS? Notice that in most cases it does so only if the pattern is vowel-consonant-vowel. That shows how consistent spelling really is, if you understand the patterns of English.

Study the word *argument*. It comes from *argue,* not *arge.* The rule for adding common endings that we stated in Chapter 5 applies to all the above words.

Silent *e* is also a clue to the pronunciation of *c.* We'll discuss that use in Chapter 9. But before we go on, let's reword our silent *e* rule for easy remembering, and practice using it.

Pattern for adding silent e: *If a word has a long vowel sound and that LVS isn't followed by a consonant and then another vowel, an* e *is usually written in after the vowel to show that it's an LVS.*

If a word has a soft g sound, and it isn't followed by a vowel, an e *is usually added after the g to show the sound.*

When adding endings to a word that has a silent e *at the end, the* e *is usually dropped if the ending starts with a vowel, but is kept if the ending starts with a consonant, so that the VCV pattern is kept.* (Silent *e* following a soft *g* sound is normally dropped only before the vowel *i.* We'll explain why in Chapter 11.)

Bear in mind that both the doubling of consonants after a short vowel sound and the adding of silent *e* after a long vowel sound occur regularly only in native English words—though, as we'll see later, the pattern does somewhat influence the other two types of words, Invasion words and Latin- and Greek-derived words. And even in native English there are some exceptions, for instance the words ending in *-ld* (*gold, bold,* etc.).

Demons to learn:

dying—dyeing
smooth—soothe

nine—ninety—nineteen—ninth
wholly (whole + -ly)
courageous, outrageous
changeable, chargeable
prestigious, religious
vengeance, acreage
exaggerate, marriage (marry + -age)

The ending -*y* sometimes retains the -*e* before it and sometimes doesn't. That will be discussed in Chapter 19.

A number of words that have the soft *g* sound are spelled with *j*. We'll look at those words in Chapter 11.

EXERCISE 21

Find the misspelled words and spell them correctly, checking your corrections to make sure that you've followed the pattern for adding silent *e*.

broker	disclosure	protrudeing
measurable	approveal	iceing
humanely	distastful	hireling
spinal	amazement	untimly
pokeing	arrangment	wipeing
guileless	behaveior	spiteful
kitemaker	chafeing	introduceing
primeary	reassureance	fortuneate
livlihood	surely	

EXERCISE 22

Follow the instructions for the previous exercise.

changeing	oblige	rageing
changeling	infringment	spongier
aging	imageine	stageing
forges	pageant	twinges
carrage	vegtable	voyaging
hughly		

EXERCISE 23

Add the indicated endings to the following words. Then check your spelling against the answers at the end of the book.

nature + -ally

plane + -ed

prophesy + -ed

where + -ever

value + -able

plan + -ed

strict + -ly

un- + doubt + -ed + -ly

family + -ar

state + -ment

hero + -s

hope + -ing

tire + -ed

shine + -ing

true + -ly

hop + -ing

lay + -ed

study + -ing

stop + -ed

skin + -ing

use + -ing

become + -ing

believe + -ing

believe + -ed

boundary + -s

buoy + -ant

climb + -ed

decide + -ed

desire + -able

dormitory + -s

employ + -ed

employee + -s

fraternity + -s

EXERCISE 24

Learn the spellings of the following words. Are they exceptions to the rule? Tell why or why not. (This question is hard to answer. Don't be discouraged if you get it wrong.)

pigeon

pageant

geography

gorgeous

hygiene

outrageous

surgeon

urgent

Chapter Summary

Native English words follow three basic patterns of spelling:

1. Each sound is represented by a letter unless there's a reason for doing otherwise.
2. Spellings follow the pattern LVS = VCV, SVS = VCCV.
3. Silent *e* is added at the end of a word with a long vowel sound to satisfy the pattern LVS = VCV.

In addition:

4. If a word has a soft *g* sound, and it isn't followed by a vowel, an *e* is usually added after the *g* to indicate that sound.
5. When adding endings to a word that has a silent *e* at the end, the *e* is usually dropped if the ending starts with a vowel, but is kept if the ending starts with a consonant, so that the VCV pattern is kept. (*E* following *g* is an exception.)

Words to Learn

List the heavy-type words you can't spell, as well as the words misspelled in the exercises.

PART III

IRREGULARITIES IN NATIVE ENGLISH WORDS

8

The Consonant Sound z

Most consonants are spelled exactly the way they sound, in native English words as well as in Invasion and Latin- and Greek-derived words. But there are several ways to spell both the z and s sounds. This chapter will concentrate on z.

Back in Chapter 5, we found the pattern for spelling the z sound at the end of a plural noun: either -s or -es, depending on what comes before it (*arms, armies*). We also saw that third-person present-tense verbs take the -s ending (she *visits*). Review the pattern for spelling these endings (see pages 25–30).

Learn the following three words with z-sound endings that don't seem to be plural but take that plural -s anyway:

scissors   towards   summons

1. z sound at word beginnings

Think of all the words that begin with a z sound. Here's a partial list to start you off:

zip	**zone**	**zest**
zinc	**zoo**	**zealot**
zebra	**zero**	**zipper**

Did you find any words that begin with the spelling s for the z sound? Write your own rule for words that begin with a z sound: _____

_____.

2. When to double z

The z sound is usually doubled at the end of a one-syllable

45

word. (Review the rule and examples in Chapter 6.) In addition, there's another clue to doubling *z*. Look at these words:

drizzle	**puzzle**	**dazzle**
causal	**nasal**	**disposal**

Fill in the pattern:

If a *z* sound comes before an *-le* ending, it's spelled ____. Before an *-al* Latin-derived ending, it's spelled ____. (For more about *-le,* see Chapter 13.)

Here are all the *zz* words in common use. Notice that there are only two words (*fizz and frizz*) that are also part of longer words ending in the *le* sound. Learn them. Then, to know if the ending is spelled *-zzle* or *-sal* you have only to decide if the little word it's tacked onto is one of these two. If not, and it's a real word (*cause, dispose*), spell the ending *-sal.*

buzz		**buzzard**	
fizz	**fizzle**		
frizz	**frizzled**		**frizzy**
fuzz			**fuzzy**
	grizzled		**grizzly**
	sizzle	**blizzard**	**dizzy**
jazz			**jazzy**
	frazzle	**gizzard**	
	dazzle		
	drizzle		
	embezzle	**fezzes**	
	guzzle		**piazza***
	muzzle	**quizzes**	**quizzical**
	nozzle		
	nuzzle		
	puzzle		
	sizzle	**whizzes**	

---

*Piazza is an Invasion word, sometimes pronounced "piatza." It rhymes with *pizza.*

The following are the only words in common use that end with an undoubled -*z:*

topaz   fez   quiz   whiz   adz

Notice that *fez, quiz,* and *whiz* have a doubled *z* before endings. They are the only words of their type.

The following are the only words with a *z* sound at the end that are spelled -*s,* other than regular plural-noun and present-tense-verb endings:

as   was   his   ours   theirs   afterwards
alms   divers (adj.)*   **pampas**

Most other words that have a *z* sound at the end are spelled -*se* or -*ze.*

3. *z* sound combined with long *a* sound

Think of all the single-syllable words you know that have a long *a* sound before or after the *z* sound. How are they usually spelled?

blaze   craze   daze   gaze
civilization   utilization   azalea   zany

Write the rule: Before or after a long *a* sound, the *z* sound

_____.

Learn these exceptions, which invaded from Norman and more recent French:

braise   chaise   raise   praise

Also learn the spelling of **maize,** which comes from an Indian word.

---

*This word means *various* and is sometimes used instead of the more common *diverse,* which means *unlike.* You might enjoy comparing the two words—and their pronunciations—in a dictionary.

These demon words are Latin- and Greek-derived:

accusation	**improvisation**
mosaic	**prosaic**

Notice that accuse and improvise—used with the above endings (or any other endings)—are the only common words that spell the *za* sound *-sa*. All other words that end in the *za* sound + ending are spelled -*za* + ending.

4. z sound plus short a sound

Look at these words, in which the *z* sound comes before a short *a* sound:

plaza   recognizance   wizard

Can you think of other words with the *z* + short *a* sound? Write the rule. _____
_____.

The only common exceptions are words ending in *-se* to which an ending is added that begins with a short *a* sound:

arousal   causal   disposal   malfeasance

and the following demons:

thousand   rosary   disaster   partisan

5. z sound plus short i sound

Study the following words and find the rule:

imposition	**deposition**	**inquisition**
exquisite	**requisite**	**transit**
deposit	**visit**	**rosin**

Rule: If a short *i* sound follows a *z* sound, _____

_____.

Exceptions: Words beginning with *z* (*zinnia, zipper, zigzag*); words ending in *z* + *-ing* (*sizing, whizzing,* etc.); and *quizzical*.

If you remember this rule and the previous ones, you'll never get confused again in spelling words ending *-sition* and *-zation*.

When you use this rule, make sure you're pronouncing and hearing your words correctly. *Deposit* has a short *i* sound. *Magazine* and similar words have a long *e* sound. The ending *-ing* also has a long *e* sound.

6. *-ize* and *-ise*

Look at the following words. With your pencil, show where each word is accented. In which words is the ending spelled *-ize*?

agonize	**memorize**	**criticize**	**homogenize**
oxidize	**realize**	**idolize**	**galvanize**
comprise	**revise**	**despise**	**demise**

Can you write a rule for this pattern? If the syllable that sounds like *ize* is a(n) _____

_____, it's spelled *-ize*.

If it's an accented final syllable, it's spelled _____.

There are only a few common words (other than plural nouns) with a *z* sound in an *unaccented final syllable* that aren't spelled with *-ze*. Here's the first group to learn. You'll remember them quickly if you know the clue that *-vise* and *-cise* are Latin roots, not endings, and that, for the first-column words, *-ise* is not a Latin ending, but part of the word. For example, *chast* without *ise* isn't a word. In most cases, this is a good way to test whether an ending is *-ize* or *-ise*.

-ise	-vise	-cise	-s(e)
chastise	televise	excise (adj.)	divers (adj.)
advertise	improvise	exercise	metamorphose
compromise	supervise	exorcise	paraphrase
merchandise			turquoise
enterprise			
franchise			

If you memorize the spelling of the words in the first three columns, you'll be able to correctly spell every other commonly used word with a long i + z ending -*ize*. When adding an ending to any word, remember to follow the pattern: don't change the spelling of the small word, except to drop the silent e when necessary.

7. -*wise*

Another group of unaccented -*ise* words is the group that combines the native English ending -*wise* with other words. These include:

likewise   otherwise   sidewise   clockwise

These words are distinctive enough that you'll spell them correctly if you listen to how they're put together.

8. -*ism*

The Invasion ending -*ism* is always spelled with s, never z.

criticism   antagonism   pluralism

9. Other spellings of the z sound

There are only eight words in which a z sound is spelled *ss*. The only way to learn to spell these words is to practice seeing, saying, writing, and proofreading them. You can always spell them correctly if you say the *z* sound as if it were *s* for spelling purposes.

> **brassiere**
> **dessert** (check a dictionary if you confuse this with
>   desert)
> **dissolve**
> **hussar** (some people pronounce the *z* sound *s*)
> **hussy** (some people pronounce the *z* sound *s*)
> **possess, dispossess, possessive, possession, possessor,**
>   **prepossessing**
> **renaissance** (some people pronounce the *z* sound *s*)
> **scissors**

There's only one *z* word spelled *sc*:

discern

Some people pronounce the *sc* with a soft *s* sound.

In addition, the *z* sound is sometimes part of the sound spelled with an *x,* which we'll look at more closely in Chapter 12.

If you hear a *z* sound and it's covered by none of the previous patterns or exceptions, you'll almost always be right if you spell it with an *s.*

Here are some commonly used words spelled with the letter *z.* Have someone test your spelling of them and memorize the misspelled words.

doze	**cozy**	**amazon**	**magazine**	
fez	**frenzy**	**horizon**	**razor**	
ooze		**citizen**	**enzyme**	**bulldoze**
prize				**eczema**
size				

quiz   trapeze
seize
squeeze
breeze
freeze
froze
sneeze
whiz
gauze

Notice that if you know how to spell these words, you can correctly spell the words that include them: *haphazard, freezer, frozen, frenzied, trapezoid,* etc.

EXERCISE 25

Find the misspelled words and spell them correctly.

sodiac   televizing
zeppelin   proposal
rozary   merchandise
realization   trapesoidal
brazier   discern
maise   excema
quizzed   haphazzard
crazily   wizard
buzword   horizon
exercize   enzyme
criticize   resistor
topaze   silch

Chapter Summary

1. At a word's beginning, the *z* sound is always spelled *z*.
2. *Z* is usually doubled at the end of one-syllable words and before the *-le* ending.

3. Other than in plural nouns and third-person singular verbs, most words that end in the *z* sound are spelled *-se* or *-ze*.
4. The *z* sound before or after long *a* is usually spelled *z*.
5. The *z* sound before a short *a* sound is usually spelled *z*, unless the short *a* is part of a word ending.
6. The *z* sound before a short *i* sound is usually spelled *s*.
7. If the ending *-ize* is part of a Latin root it's spelled *-ise*. If it's a suffix (shown by the fact that it's an unaccented final syllable), it's spelled *-ize*.
8. The endings *-wise* and *-ism* are always spelled with *s*.
9. In most other cases the *z* sound is spelled *s*.

Words to Learn

List the heavy-type words you can't spell, as well as the words misspelled in the exercises.

9

The Consonant Sound s

The *s* sound is a difficult one because it is usually written one of two ways, *s* or *c*, and has several other peculiarities as well. For instance, a common *s*-sound ending is *'s*, to show possession. (If you have trouble knowing when to use the apostrophe, consult a good grammar book.) But there are some patterns to the spelling of the *s* sound.

1. s sound before *a, o, u*, or a consonant

A bit of history helps us find our first generalization. In early English the sound *s* was never written *c*; that letter was reserved for *k* sounds:

cut   come   color

The words that spell the *s* sound with a *c* are mostly derived from French and Latin:

cent	malice	viceroy	civic	cistern
cemetery	certain	necessary	cycle	cymbal

In all of these Invasion words, the letter that follows is *e, i,* or *y*. Therefore, if the letter that follows is *not e, i,* or *y*, the *s* sound is spelled _____.

Note that an *s* sound before an *e, i,* or *y* can be spelled *either s* or *c*.

consensus   similar   ceiling   symbol

2. s sound at word beginnings

Most words that begin with an *s* sound in an *unaccented syllable* are spelled with an *s* (*sin-cere'*, *se-rene'*). Learn these exceptions that begin with *c* (they are the only common exceptions to this pattern):

cerebral	cessation	civilian	cement
cerebrum	centennial	civility	cigar
ceramic	centrifugal	celestial	citation
certificate	centurion	celebrity	cyclonic
circuitous			cylindrical
circumference			

Words that begin with an *accented syllable* follow no particular pattern except the one already discussed—that if the second letter is *a, o, u,* or a consonant, the first letter is an *s*.

EXERCISE 26

Cross off all of the above words that come from words that *are* accented on the first syllable. Now you need memorize only the few that are left. (The answers are at the end of the book.)

3. s sound doublings

Study the following words:

decision   recipe   dulcimer   accede

Can you think of *any* words in which the *s* sound is spelled *cc*? (Notice that, in a word like *accede,* the first *c* is a *k* sound.) The pattern shown above, which has no exceptions, can be stated thus: *If the s sound is spelled with a c, the c is never doubled.*

In short native English words the *s* is doubled after most short vowel sounds according to the patterns studied in Chapter 6:

moss   lass   kiss   gossip

It's also doubled in some words that come from Latin and other languages:

colossal   aggressive   association   assassin

One common doubling of *s* occurs when a Latin prefix ending in *s* comes smack up against a root beginning in *s*:

assume   dissent   essay

More about that in Part IV.

Learn these homonyms:

canvas—canvass   counsel—council   vice—vise

4. s sound after long vowel sound

Most words with an *s* sound after a long vowel sound spell it *c* (or *c* + silent *e* at the end of a word):

truce   nice   bracing   induce   license

That's because an -*s* after an LVS is usually pronounced -*z*:

miser   chose   wise   use

5. s sound word endings

In addition to the plural noun and present-tense verb endings that sometimes sound like the *s* sound (*cats, baths, stuffs*), several English and Latin endings also end in that sound. When you hear the following, they're always spelled the same:

> *-ess* (as in **impress, address, mistress**)
> *-less* (as in **witless, nevertheless**)
> *-ness* (as in **wilderness, calmness**)

Don't confuse the short *e* sound in *-ess, -less,* and *-ness* with the vowel sound in *-ous,* which is discussed in Part IV. It's a slightly different sound.

Two other common Latin endings, in addition to *-ous,* have a soft *s* sound: the first can be spelled *-ence* or *-ense*; the second can be spelled *-ce* or *-se*. We'll hold those problem endings for Part IV.

Demon to memorize: **embarrass**

6. s sound before t sound

In many words, a *t* sound comes right after the *s* sound:

western   masthead   costly   cistern   mystery

Pattern: The *st* sound combination is *always* spelled

_____.

If you can't hear that *st* sound clearly, open a dictionary to words beginning with *st* and say them slowly aloud. Some people drop the *t* in words like *against* and *instant*. If you do, try to exaggerate your enunciation when you're spelling.

7. s sound followed by silent t

Some words do have a silent *t* sound between the *s* and an *l* or *n* sound. Memorize the spelling of these words so that you can remember to put in the *t*:

apostle   hustle   moisten   fasten

jostle	rustle	christen	hasten
bristle	bustle	glisten	chasten
whistle	pestle	listen	chestnut
epistle	nestle		
gristle	trestle	mistletoe	
thistle	wrestle		

Notice that some of the above words ending in -en come from smaller words that end in -t or -te. It will help you remember their spelling. This follows the primary rule of English spelling: *To spell a big word that comes from a small word, you keep the spelling of the small word (except for dropping the silent e that makes a VCV pattern).* If you've forgotten the rule, review Chapter 4 now.

8. Silent c after s sound

An annoying number of words have a silent *c* after the *s* sound. Your best bet is to memorize these words, since they're a lot of fun to use. (Remember that bigger words made from these words are also spelled with an *sc*.)

science	ascend	abscess
scene	transcend	plebiscite
scent	descend	ascetic
scepter	disciple	discipline
scintillate	obscene	fascinate
scion	oscilloscope	oscillate
scissors	proscenium	eviscerate
scythe	rescind	resuscitate
scenario	susceptible	crescent
muscle	miscible	nascent
	irascible	miscellaneous
	discernible	

Many of the words in the second and third columns are made

up of Latin prefixes that end in *s* and roots that begin in *c*. That's why they're spelled the way they are. For example, susceptible is *sus* + *cept* + ending. More about this in Chapter 15.

In addition, there is a Latin *-esce* ending that's always accented. Sometimes it has an *-ent* or *-ence* ending added on (always spelled *-en,* not *-an*). You can learn to hear it. It's in the following common words:

acquiesce	**adolescent**
coalesce	**convalescence**
effervesce	**quiescent**
	fluorescent
	obsolescent
	phosphorescent

9. Silent *p* before *s* sound

There are just a few common words (and the words that are built up from them) that start with a silent *p* in front of the *s* sound. These words all come from Greek. Memorize them:

psalm		
pseudo	**pseudonym**	**pseudopod** (etc.)
psyche	**psychic**	
psycho	**psychoanalysis**	**psychosomatic** (etc.)
psychiatry		

10. *s* sound followed by silent *ch*

There is only one common English word in which the *s* sound has a silent *ch* after it:

schism (pronounced either *skism* or *sism*)

There are only two common cases of a silent *w* after the *s* sound:

sword   answer

11. s sound spelled z

A few common words spell the *s* sound with the letter *z:*

chintz   quartz   waltz

12. s sound spelled c

The Latin root *cede* appears in many words:

precede   concede   recede   accede   (etc.)

Learn these demon exceptions:

supersede: (the only word spelled *sede*)
succeed, proceed, exceed (the only three words spelled *ceed*)

The root of the word never changes its spelling when an ending is added:

preceding   superseded

except for these two exceptions:

procedure   procedural

In the huge study of English spelling referred to earlier, it was found that the *s* sound is spelled *s* in three-quarters of all words. So if in doubt, and you can't find a rule or spelling that you're familiar with, guess at *s*.

EXERCISE 27

Correct the incorrectly spelled words.

centrifugal	aggressive	hussler
centimental	progresive	acid
circuitous	clasical	massive
sychotic	asinine	nameles
misile	anxioussness	sassy
crestent	system	supersede
whittless	politeness	consensus
missiletoe	occillate	senter
scism	crass	
fluorescent	consist	

Chapter Summary

1. Before *a, o, u,* or a consonant the *s* sound is almost always spelled *s*. Before *e, i,* or *y,* it is spelled *s* or *c*.
2. Most words that begin with the *s* sound in an unaccented syllable spell the sound *s*.
3. The *s* sound is never doubled if it is spelled *c*.
4. After an LVS, the *s* sound is usually spelled *c*.
5. Common word endings are *-less, -ness,* and *-ess* (which has a vowel sound different from *-ous*).
6. The *st* sound combination is always spelled *st*.
7. If in doubt, spell the *s* sound *s*.

Words to Learn

List the heavy-type words you can't spell, as well as the words misspelled in the exercises.

10

The Consonant Sounds *v* and *k*

The consonant sounds *v* and *k* cause needless trouble to poor spellers who haven't figured out their patterns of use. Once you understand them, many spelling problems disappear.

The *v* sound

Most people who have trouble with *v* do so because one of the first words they learn is *of*. But that's the *only* word in English that spells the *v* sound with an *f*! With that in mind, you'll never have trouble with *v* again.

There are only three common *v* words with a silent *l* in front of the *v* (in addition to all the words that change *-lf* to *-lv* to form plurals; see Chapter 5). Memorize them.

> **calve** (meaning "to give birth to a calf")
> **salve**
> **halve** (meaning "to cut in half")

The *k* sound

Most of our words use the letter *c* for a *k* sound. *K* was always preferred for native English words, although there weren't many of them, so think of *k* as a native English letter. *C* is an import that arrived with Invasion and Renaissance words. If you aren't sure of a spelling of the sound *k* you're most likely to get it right if you spell it *c*. However, the use of *k* does follow some clear patterns.

Study these four columns of words. Each column shows a different pattern in which the letter *k* is used for the sound *k*.

in front of *e, i, or y*	*after a* *consonant*	*after an* *LVS*	*after an* *SVS*
keep	thank	wake	sock
clear	mark	like	smack
kestral	sulk	stroke	pick
kine	chunk	meek	wreck
hanky	brisk	bleak	panic
kindergarten	mink	squeak	tropic
cool	talk	week	basic

Can you complete the patterns?

1. At the beginning of a word, the *k* sound is spelled_____ before the vowels *e, i,* and *y*.

The reason for this is simple, once you remember that in Invasion and Latin-derived words, the *s* sound is spelled *c* before the vowels *e, i,* and *y*. To make sure that you pronounce a word correctly if you see it in print, *k* was adopted as the better alternative for the *k* sound in these situations.

Before a vowel *other* than *e, i,* or *y,* there are very few words that spell the *k* sound *k*. Their unique appearance makes them easy to memorize. They're all listed below. (The *k* sound is spelled *c* in all others words in which the *k* sound comes before *a, o, u,* or a consonant.)

okay	kangaroo	alkaline
ukulele	kaleidoscope	bazooka
askance	kaput	mazurka
skate	kazoo	paprika
skulk		polka
skull		swastika
skunk		vodka

Remember the rule that words made up of little words don't change the spelling of the little words:

bulkhead   cookbook   bookkeeper   remarkable

If you keep the above thoughts in mind, you'll be right most of the time in your spelling of a *k* sound before a vowel sound.

2. At the end of a native English word, after a consonant sound the *k* sound is spelled _____.

Some native English words of that type are:

       coxcomb   pancake   outcrop

Latin-derived words spell the *k* sound with a *c* even when it follows a consonant sound. This rarely occurs at the end of a word. Part IV will help you recognize Latin- and Greek-derived words.

A few words that aren't native English, but look it, are:

zinc	**sarcasm**	**rancor**	**rascal**	**rescue**
talc	**talcum**		**tincture**	**arctic***

Memorize the spelling of these words, and you'll have little trouble spelling the *k* sound after a consonant sound.

3. At the end of a native English word, the *k* sound is spelled _____ after a long vowel sound.

It's rare for Latin-derived words to have a *k* sound after a long vowel sound *unless* the LVS ends the prefix. In the following words, we've separated the prefix from the rest of the word to clarify this point:

    re-consider   pre-condition   anti-climactic

EXERCISE 28

Consult Appendix A and fill in all the prefixes that end in a long vowel sound.

---

*Some people pronounce *arctic* without the *k* sound. You'll always spell it correctly if you enunciate the *k* sound.

4. At the end of a native English word, the *k* sound is spelled _____ after a short vowel sound.

Almost all the one-syllable words having a *k* sound after a short vowel are native English:

black   suck   trick

A number of two-syllable words are also native English, such as:

thicket   knuckle   speckle

Many Latin- and Greek-derived words have a *k* sound after an SVS, and it's usually spelled *c*. In fact, *-ic* is a common Greek suffix. But the few *-ic* words that have been made into verbs always add an English *k* before endings beginning in *i, e,* or *y* so that the reader doesn't mistakenly pronounce an *s* sound for the *c*.

panic	**panicking**	**panicky**	**panics**	**panicked**
picnic	**picnicking**	**picnicker**	**picnics**	**picnicked**

When you meet an SVS + *k* sound combination, try to decide whether the word is native or comes from Latin or Greek—and then note whether it's being used as a verb.

5. The Greek *ch*

Some Greek-derived words spell the *k* sound *ch*. Here are the most common of them. Notice that the *ch* is part of a *root,* not a suffix. (Ache is not from the Greek, but we include it here for you to memorize.)

chasm	**scheme**	**melancholy**	**monarch**
chronic	**school**	**mechanic**	**archaic**
chaos	**schedule**	**technical**	**architect**
chameleon	**scholar**	**orchid**	**anarchy**

chord	schooner	bronchial	archetype
chorus	schizophrenia	dichotomy	
character		orchestra	
chemical	epoch	alchemy	
chlorine	stomach	anchor	
christen	ocher	lichen	
chrome	ache	psychology	
chromatic	echo		

Notice that all the words in column four have the same root: *arch*. If you learn the words in columns one through three, you should be able to spell other words that contain the same roots, for example:

chronicle	chronometer	chronology	chronological
chronically	synchronize	anachronism	chronoscope
chloride	hydrochloric	chloroform	chlorophyll
psyche	psychic	psychotic	psychosomatic
aching	heartache	headache	toothache

6. *k* sound after prefixes ending in the *k* sound

A number of Greek- and Latin-derived words combine a prefix ending in *c* (*ac-*, *ec-*, *oc-*, *suc-*) with a root word beginning in the *k* sound. Those words are spelled with two *c*'s in a row. Here are a few:

account	ecclesiastical	occupation
accustom	succumb	occur
accurate	succor	occasion

They're easy to spell if you separate roots from prefixes as you sound out the words you're spelling. We'll show you how in Part IV.

7. *k* sound demons to memorize

a. A few Invasion words are spelled *cc*:

yucca	raccoon	staccato	toccata	broccoli
piccolo	tobacco	succor	moccasin	buccaneer

b. A few native English words have a silent *l* before the *k* (it used to be pronounced):

balk	chalk	talk	folk
walk	stalk	calk	yolk

c. Some words that are recent transplants from French or Spanish spell the *k* sound *qu* or, if at the end, *-que*:

mannequin	croquet	mosquito	unique
torque	pique	oblique	opaque

d. The word **saccharin** comes from a Greek word, *sakcharon,* meaning *sugar.* It's the only English word with two *c*'s and an *h* in a row.

EXERCISE 29

Correct the misspelled words.

nukleus	calkulate
across	clorine
accept	ache
artical	sacharin
attacced	unique
sacrifise	syncronize
ridiculous	psychology
kavalry	tobaco
docktor	picknicking
sinserely	knuckle
course	rascle
unique	bookeeping
calc	

Chapter Summary

1. The sound *v* is spelled *v* in all cases but one, the word *of.*
2. At the beginning of a word, the sound *k* is spelled *k* before the vowels *e, i,* and *y.* Otherwise, most of the time it's spelled *c.*
3. At the end of a native English word, the *k* sound is spelled *ck* after an SVS and *k* + silent *e* after an LVS. After a consonant it's spelled *k.*
4. In Latin-derived words, the *k* sound is usually spelled *c.*
5. In Greek-derived words, the *k* sound is sometimes spelled *ch.*

Words to Learn

After someone has tested your knowledge of the words in heavy type in this chapter, write your demons here along with the words you got wrong in Exercise 29.

11

The Consonant Sound *j*

The most common way of writing the *j* sound is with the letter *g*. In fact, the letter *j* is used less than one-fourth of the time. However, there is a pattern for when the *j* sound is written *j*. See if you can find it. (*Hint:* The pattern is similar to one we found for when the *s* sound is written *s*.)

jam	**job**	**jump**
ajar	**jocular**	**justify**
ejaculate	**pejorative**	**subjugate**

Pattern for writing the *j* sound with *j*: In most cases, write the *j* sound with *j* before the letters _____
_____.

Only common exceptions:

algae   **margarine**

1. When the *j* sound is written *g*

The following words offer a clue to the most common use of *g* for *j*. See if you can find it. (*Hint:* In Latin-derived and Invasion words, the relationship between *j* and *g* is similar to that between *s* and *c*.)

gist	**fungi**	**gyrate**
urgent	**gesture**	**gypsy**

Pattern for substituting *g* for the *j* sound: In imported words, just as the *s* sound is written *c* before _____

_____, the *j* sound is most often written ____ in front of those letters.

This is *not* true of native English words. Memorize the common native words in which *e* or *i* follows the *j* sound:

jest	jewel	jelly	jeer	jet	jealous	jeep
jib	jiggle	jingle	jilt	jive	jiffy	jimmy

There are also a few imported exceptions, the majority containing the Latin root *ject,* which is always spelled with a *j*:

reject   conjecture   subject   objective (etc.)

In addition, these common words should be memorized:

jeopardy   jejune   jettison

To help people read the *j* sound correctly when it's spelled *g,* the silent *e* is left in before *a, o, u,* or a consonant.

courageous	changeable	dungeon	gorgeous
arrangement	advantageous	geography	encouragement

But it's not needed before *e, i,* or *y* since *g* always has the *j* sound in these instances.

legion   allegiance   changing   merger   spongy

2. *j* sound before the long *u* sound

A number of words seem to have a *j* sound before a long *u* sound, when the sound is really a *d.* Memorize these words, exaggerating their enunciation:

arduous	**modulate**	**gradual**
deciduous	**undulate**	**residual**
assiduous	**graduate**	**individual**
credulous	**educate**	**verdure**
modulus	**glandular**	**grandeur**
fraudulent	**pendulum**	**procedure**
	schedule	

3. *j* sound word endings

The letter *j* never ends a word. Notice how the *j* sound is written at the end of native English words:

After an LVS	After a consonant	After an SVS
rage	flange	hedge, hedging
stage	urge	drudge, drudgery
huge	divulge	bridge, abridging
wager	sponge	edge, edgy

Pattern: The sound *j* at the end of a native English word is written ____ after a long vowel sound or a consonant, and ____ after a short vowel sound. As with other English words, if an ending is added, the spelling of the word (changes, doesn't change) _____, and the silent *e* is (dropped, kept) _____ before a vowel.

Once you understand this pattern, you should never again have trouble spelling these native English words:

fidget   gadget   bludgeon   cudgel   grudging

There are only a few two-syllable native English words that end in the *j* sound (other than those derived from one-syllable words). They're easy to memorize.

knowledge   partridge   porridge   cartridge

The British follow the same rule for endings before consonants that begin Latin suffixes as they do for those that begin English suffixes:

> judgement   acknowledgement   abridgement

But American dictionaries prefer to drop the *e* before endings like *-ment.* Memorize these examples:

> **judgment   acknowledgment   abridgment**

(Fledgling is spelled without the *e* in both countries.)

4. The *j* sound in *-age*

The Latin suffix *-age* is usually pronounced as if it were short *a* + *j* (*courage*). Many, many common verbs and nouns have this ending, for instance:

> **manage   mortgage   percentage   suffrage   envisage**

(Notice that *-age* words must have at least two syllables.) Exceptions: two common words are spelled *-ege,* and one is spelled *-ige.* Memorize them:

> **college   privilege   vestige**

5. The sound *d* before the *j* sound

Some Latin-derived words that have roots beginning with *j* start with the prefix *ad-*

> **adjust   adjective   adjourn   adjacent** (etc.)

You can't tell where the *d* ends and the *j* begins by listening to these words. However, since there's no Latin or Greek prefix that's just a short *a* sound, nearly every time you hear the combination sound short *a* + *j* at the beginning of a word, you'll be correct if you automatically spell it *adj-*. The only common exceptions are:

agenda　　agile　　agitate　　ajar

6. Two exceptions to all the patterns

Two words that have a *j* sound don't fit into any of the above discussions. Memorize them.

cordial (which is pronounced as if it were spelled *corgial*)
exaggerate (which is the only common *j*-sounded word
　　spelled with a doubled *g*)

EXERCISE 30

1. Tell what letter is inserted to keep the *g* sound hard in front of *e* and *i*:

guess　　disguise　　guitar　　guest　　guide

2. What letter or letters keep the *g* hard in the following words?

fugue　　brogue　　plague　　rogue　　fatigue

EXERCISE 31

1. Name four words that have two syllables and end in -*edge* or *idge*.
2. Name two words that have two syllables and end in -*ege*.
3. What ending do most other two-syllable words have that end in the *j* sound? (You may have found responses to (1) and (2) that are different from ours.)

EXERCISE 32

Correct the misspelled words.

huge	village	arranging
carrage	indigestible	adgile
changing	lejitimate	adgenda
vijilant	oblige	adjust
vegtable	encourageing	manadge

Chapter Summary

1. The *j* sound is usually written *j* before *a, o,* and *u,* and *g* before *e, i,* and *y*—except in native English words, which most often spell the *j* sound *j.*

2. In imported words, before an ending beginning in *a, o, u,* or a consonant, silent *e* is left in after *g* to indicate the *j* sound. It's usually dropped before *e, i,* or *y.*

3. At the end of a native English word, the sound *j* is written *-ge* after a long vowel sound or a consonant and *-dge* after a short vowel sound. If an ending is added, the helping *e* is usually dropped.

4. The Latin suffix that has the sound short *a* + *j* is almost always spelled *-age.*

5. The sound short *a* + *j* at the beginning of a word is almost always spelled *adj-.*

Words to Learn

List the heavy-type words you can't spell, as well as the words misspelled in the exercises.

12

A Double Sound Represented by One Letter: *x*

One English letter is used to represent a combination of consonant sounds: the letter *x*. Read the following words aloud and listen for the hidden sounds.

axis   **execute**   **ixnay**   **oxen**   **flux**

Pattern for the letter *x:* The letter *x* represents the consonant _____ followed immediately by the consonant _____.

1. *ks* sound word endings

The letter *x* gives trouble because, like the sounds *s* and *z*, the sound *ks* can be written several ways:

tax	**tacks**	**attacks**
flux	**flocks**	**attics**

To avoid confusion, keep in mind that the *-cks* ending is rarely used except in plurals of native English nouns and third-person singular present-tense verbs (see the discussion of the *k* sound in Chapter 10), and that the following, along with words derived from them (which we're sure you already know how to spell), are the only common English words that end in *x*:

ax	**fix**	**relax**	**matrix**
wax	**six**	**apex**	**phoenix**
lax	**mix**	**complex**	**onyx**

75

tax		annex	affix
ox		index	prefix
box	hex	reflex	appendix
fox	sex	perplex	orthodox
	vex	vortex	paradox
coax	flex	latex	lynx
hoax	flux	influx	larynx
			sphinx

2. The prefix ex-

Many Latin-derived words begin with the prefix *ex-*. There, the *ks* sound is *always* spelled *x*.

extreme   exalt   exist

When the *ks* sound comes before a vowel, as in *exalt,* we tend to pronounce it *gs*. (Don't make the mistake of inserting an extra *s* in these words after the *x*.)

Some Latin-derived words combine the prefix *ex-* with a root that begins with an *s* sound, spelled *c*:

exceed	excite	excel	except
excerpt	excess	excise	

Memorize these tricky *ex-* words. They (and the words derived from them, like *excellent*) are the only words that begin with an *eks* sound that are spelled *exc-*. Also keep in mind that an *x* rarely comes anywhere but in the prefix *ex-* in Latin-derived words. Don't spell the word *enacts* as if it were *inax*.

Here are all the commonly used words that have an *x* buried in their midst. Memorize the ones you don't know.

(ax)	*(ex)*	*(ix)*	*(ox)*	*(ux)*
axiom	next	elixir	oxide	luxury
axis	text	vixen	oxygen	juxtapose

(ax)	*(ex)*	*(ix)*	*(ox)*	*(ux)*
axle	pretext		intoxicate	buxom
laxative	context		proximity	
maxim	textile		toxic	
maximum	texture		toxin	
saxophone	inexorable			
taxi	hexagon			
taxidermy	flexible			
galaxy	dexterous			
	sextant			
	perplexity			
	reflexive			

The words *reflexive* and *perplexity* should be particularly studied. (*Reflexive* comes from *reflex,* not *reflect.*)

3. The prefix *ac-* plus the *s* sound

Notice that when the Latin prefix *ac-* comes before a word beginning with the *s* sound, an *x* sound is created. Spell these words correctly even if you think you hear *x*.

accelerator   accessible   accidentally   accept

4. Plural ending *-ics*

The plural ending *-ics* is fairly common:

genetics   mechanics   tactics   obstetrics

If you remember the first rule of English spelling (the spelling of a small word never changes when it's made longer), you'll never write *mechanix* or *tactix.*

5. A demon to memorize

There's a tricky word that defies all English spelling

patterns for the *ks* sound. It's really a *k* + *z* sound, but saying the two together quickly produces *ks*. Memorize the word:

eczema (the Latin prefix *ec* + the root *zema*)

EXERCISE 33

Correct the misspelled words.

expense	egsplanation	exercise	influx
ecsperience	exhorbitant	inexact	orthodocks
extremely	existence	tocsin	complex
extrordinary	exellent	deduxs	excecute
ecstension			

Chapter Summary

1. The letter *x* represents the consonant cluster *ks*.
2. Only a few words end in the letter *x*.
3. Only native English plurals and third-person-singular verbs end in the spelling *-cks*.
4. Many Latin-derived words begin with *ex-*.
5. The Latin prefix *ac-* and the suffix *-ics* are never spelled with *x*.

Words to Learn

List the heavy-type words you can't spell, as well as the words misspelled in the exercises.

13

Consonant Clusters:
qu, ng, wh, ch, sh, le

Since there are more sounds in English than there are letters to represent them, combinations of letters have been designated to stand for certain sounds. Let's examine these letter clusters and their uses.

The sound of the letters *qu*

There is no special English sound for the letter combination *qu*. Sound out these words and figure out what combination of native English consonants the cluster overlaps.

quiet   quite   required   liquid   equal

Did you figure out that the letters *qu* stand for the combination of consonants *kw*? Notice that q *without* u *has no sound; it needs the* u *after it to be complete.*

This particular combination of sounds, *kw*, never existed together in native English. (The native English word *awkward* is *awk + ward,* not *aw + kw + ard.*) All the words that have the *kw* sound came from other languages. So every time you hear the sound, it's spelled *qu*. Think of *qu* as one letter and you won't go wrong.

1. Confusion of *kw* sound with the *cu* sound

The combination of sounds made by *cu* is different from

the *kw* sound. Say these words over and over; notice how your lips change and listen for the difference:

cute	**quota**
courtier	**quarter**
cucumber	**quickly**
cure	**quark**

2. *qu* after the prefix *ac·*

Study the following words:

acquaint   acquit   acquire

These words are the only commonly used words that have a Latin root preceded by the Latin prefix *ac-*.

Notice the difference between the spelling of the above words and the following, which don't contain the prefix *ac-* but the root *aqua*:

aquatic   aquarium

Spelling really does make sense!

The sound of the letters *ng*

The letters *ng* sometimes stand for a twanging English sound that appears at the end of many native English words:

sing   rang   belong

Say these words over and over, listening to the sound. Notice that the *n* sound is said, and then the mouth is drawn back as if to begin a *g* sound—but the *g* sound is never finished.

The most common use of the special *ng* sound is in the present-tense ending *-ing*.

troubling   connecting   blacking

Learn to hear the difference between these two words:

angle (*ng* sound)　　**angel** (n + soft *g*)

When the common English endings are added to short *o* + *ng* words (and by many speakers to other *ng* words as well), sometimes an extra *g* sound is inserted to make them easier to say. Don't spell that extra *g* sound with another *g* when you're writing the words.

thronging　　longer　　strongest　　wrongly

Notice that many common words that include the special *ng* sound add that extra *g* sound for ease of speaking.

angle　　finger　　mongrel　　hunger

(You may have already noticed that no common English word is spelled with an *e* before the *ng* sound.*)

1. *ng* sound before the *k, kw,* and *g* sounds

Study the following words for their pattern:

thank	**wink**	**monk**	**sunk**	**adjunct**
anchor	**zinc**	**conch**	**uncle**	**instinct**
anguish	**jingle**	**congress**	**bungalow**	**incongruity**
banquet	**tranquil**	**conquest**	**vanquish**	**relinquish**

Pattern for *ng* sound before *k, kw,* and *g* sounds: Before a *k, kw,* or *g* sound, spell the *ng* sound _____.

2. Other *ng* words to memorize

The following words are often pronounced with an *ng*

---

*The proper noun *Bengal*, pronounced either *Ben'-gal* or *Beng'-gal*, is an import.

sound, and that may confuse you about their spelling.

conqueror   anxious   anxiety

Warning: Don't confuse the *ng* sound with the *-gn* spelling of the Latin-derived *-ign*. Say these words, and notice that they don't use the special *ng* sound, but a simple *n* sound:

benign   resign   assign   align

The *-hw* sound

As we pointed out in Chapter 2, the sound *hw*, spelled *wh*, is fast disappearing in America. But the *spelling* lingers on. The best way to get these words right is to memorize them. (Keep in mind that words that have these words in them are also spelled *wh*, for example *everywhere*.)

whack	wheat	which	whorl	why
whale	wheedle	whiff		
wharf	wheel	while		
what	wheeze	whim		
	when	whimper	whisk	whit
	where	whimsy	whiskey	white
	whet	whine	whisper	whither
	whether	whinny	whistle	whittle
	whew	whip		
	whey	whirl		
		whiz		

Memorize the only word of this type that doesn't include a familiar *wh*-beginning word:

overwhelm

1. *h* sound spelled *wh*

The words that have an *o* sound after the *hw* sound (except for *whorl*) ended up having the *w* sound dropped for ease of pronunciation. The following are the only common words of that type, and you probably know how to spell most of them already.

who   whom   whole   whoop   whore   whose

2. Silent *h*

Now's as good a time as any to learn the words that used to be pronounced with an *h* in them but aren't any longer. You must memorize the fact that they're still spelled with the *h*.

heir	**graham**	**exhaust**	**vehicle**
herb	**shepherd**	**exhibit**	**vehement**
honest	**posthumous**	**exhort**	**annihilate**
honor		**exhilarate**	
hour			

3. Homonyms to learn

The *wh* combination is used to flag a number of common homonyms. Memorize them.

which—witch	**whey—way**	**what—watt**
whale—wail	**where—wear**	**whet—wet**
whine—wine	**whit—wit**	**whether—weather**

The sounds of *ch* and *sh*

The relationship between *ch* and *sh* is like that between *c* and *s*. *Ch* is a hard, strident sound. *Sh* is a soft whisper. If you can't hear the difference right off the bat, say these words aloud, exaggerating your enunciation, until you can.

chill	shill	chip	ship
chant	shan't	crutch	crush
chuck	shuck	latch	lash
chop	shop	witch	wish

1. *ch* and *sh* word endings

Look at the last three sets of words in the above list, and at the words that follow, and pick out the formula for word endings.

after an SVS	*after a consonant*	*after an LVS**
retch	bunch	teach
catch	lurch	approach
hitch	finch	leech
scotch	porch	vouch
hutch	search	hooch

Pattern for words that end in a *ch* or *sh* sound: Words that end in the *ch* sound spell the sound ____, except after a ____, when the sound is spelled ____. Words that end in the *sh* sound spell that final *sh* sound ____.

Notice that the extra *t* before the *ch* isn't dropped even when a common word ending is added, in line with our first rule of English spelling:

crutches   satchel   twitched

Exceptions: A few common words don't insert the *t* when the *ch* sound ends a word:

rich   which   much   such
duchess   bachelor   breeches

(*Breeches* is pronounced as if it were spelled *britches*).

---

*These double-vowel sounds will be discussed in Chapters 19 and 20. For now, just notice that long vowel sounds before *ch* are always written with two letters.

2. *sh* sound spelled *ci*

There are several Latin endings which have the *sh* and *ch* sounds in them (for instance, *-tion, -sion, -cious, -tue,* and *-tuous*). We'll look at them in Chapter 16.

In addition, in words imported from other languages, the *sh* sound is always spelled simply *c* before a long *e* sound.

appreciate   appreciable   associate   fiduciary

3. *sh* sound spelled *ch* in imported words

In French the *sh* sound is spelled *ch*. That's why French imports like **chef, chute,** and **crochet** are spelled that way. Watch for these *ch* words as you read. Most of them *begin* with the *sh* sound; the few common exceptions are:

brochure   machine   ricochet   nonchalant   parachute
echelon   gauche   mustache   pistachio

Also learn the word **ache,** which is spelled with *ch* and pronounced as if it were spelled *ake*. (Greek-derived words also spell the *k* sound *ch*. See Chapter 10.)

4. *sh* sound as a slurred *s*

A few common words slur the *s* sound so that it sounds like *sh*—simply because it is easier than pronouncing the *s* sound. That happens mostly before the letter *u*:

surely   cynosure   censure   insure
sugar   sensual   nausea*

---

*Nausea is shown in *Webster's New Collegiate Dictionary* (8th ed.) as having four correct pronunciations: nau´-*zee*-a, nau´-*sha*, nau´-*see*-a, and nau´-*zha*. We learned it as nau´-*zha*.

5. Uncommon spellings of *sh* and *ch* sounds

The *sh* sound is spelled *sc* in just a few easy-to-learn words:

conscience	prescience	omniscience
crescendo	fascism	
conscious	luscious	

The *ch* sound is spelled *c* in the following Italian-derived words:

cello	concerto

The sound of the ending *-le*

The sound of the ending *-le* is not the same as that of the letter *l.* Compare the two in these words:

sapling	apple	applejack
doubtless	bottle	bottler
fondly	candle	candling
allow	edible	measles

Do you hear that the words in Column one have a simple *l* sound, while those in Columns two and three have a very short, almost swallowed *uh* sound in front of the *l* sound? If you learn to pronounce *-le* correctly when you see it, and to hear it in words in which it appears, you'll usually spell it correctly. (Notice that the Latin endings *-ible* and *-able* have that sound.)

1. Exceptions in spelling the *uhl* sound

A few short native-looking words spell the *uhl* sound *-al,* *-il, -ol,* and *-el.* There are so few of them, you should be able to remember them and to spell all the others *-le.* Here are the most common.

-al:	medal	metal	petal	bridal	
-il:	devil	evil	pupil	weevil	
-ol:	pistol				
-el:	chattel	easel	chisel	shovel	mussel
	mantel	weasel	shrivel	grovel	yodel
	tassel	vessel	swivel	novel	
	hazel		drivel	model	

Note that other *-al* words don't have that swallowed *-uh + l* sound:

final   rascal   original   equal

If you don't hear the difference, try saying the above words with the *-le* ending:

fine-le   rask-le   origin-le   equ-le

Do it over and over until you can sense the difference. Then learn to pronounce your words carefully for spelling purposes.

Don't confuse the *-le* ending with the *-ile* Latin ending (in words like *missile*). In these endings, you can hear the short vowel sound (or should be able to if you're pronouncing the word carefully). The endings *-tial* and *-cial* (as in *partial* and *social*) *do* contain a sound that's very close to the *uhl* sound. But since there's always a *sh* sound in front of the *uhl* sound, you should have no trouble recognizing these as Latin endings.

2. Homonyms

Memorize the following:

bridle—bridal   meddle—medal

muscle—mussel   mantle—mantel

The sounds of the letter combination *th*

The letter combination *th* stands for two separate sounds that don't have letters to represent them—a soft sound (as in *thick*) and a hard one (as in *then*). We include them here to make our discussion of consonant sounds complete. But since they're both spelled the same way, spellers rarely have trouble spelling either sound.

Only one common word spells the sound *t* with *th*:

thyme

EXERCISE 34

Correct the misspelled words.

amongst	quite
arithmetic	acqua
yacht	acquitted
wholely	aquisitive
whitch	refusal
thorough	respectable
strenth	criticle
ingkblot	slinking
drivle	angle
sandwich	angkle
quarter	

Chapter Summary

1. *Qu*, which stands for the sound cluster *kw*, is always written as if it were one letter. The *u* is never dropped.
2. Before a *k, kw,* or *g* sound, the *ng* sound is written *n*.
3. Only a few words still pronounce the *hw* sound, but many keep its *wh* spelling. In addition, a few words that begin with the sound *h* are spelled *wh-*.
4. Words that end in the *ch* sound spell the sound *-ch*

except after a short vowel sound, in which case the sound is spelled -*tch*.

5. The *sh* sound never changes its spelling in native American words, but is spelled irregularly in imported words.

6. The ending -*le* has a distinctive sound, when said correctly, that distinguishes it from -*al* and -*ile* endings. Most words that end with the distinctive -*le* sound (*uhl*) are spelled -*le* and drop the silent *e* when adding endings.

Words to Learn

List the heavy-type words you can't spell, as well as the words misspelled in the exercises.

14

Silent Consonants and Other Demons

The few English words that have lost the sounds of some of their consonants, but are still spelled the way they *used* to be pronounced, trip up even the best spellers. There's no shortcut around them. They just have to be memorized. We'll list the most common of them and suggest that you have someone test you so that you can ignore the demons you already know how to spell correctly. (We've scattered some of these tricksters in other chapters, but most are repeated here.)

Silent b: **debt, doubt, subtle**
aplomb, bomb, climb, comb, crumb, dumb, jamb, lamb, limb, numb, plumb, succumb, thumb, tomb, womb

Silent c: **indict, czar, muscle**

Silent ch: **yacht**

Silent g: **gnarled, gnash, gnat, gnaw, gnome, gnu**
phlegm, diaphragm
deign, feign, reign
campaign, arraign
sign, align, assign, benign, consign, design, malign, resign
ensign, foreign, sovereign
cologne, champagne, impugn

Silent h: **rhythm, rhyme, rhapsody, rheostat, rhetoric, rheumatic, rhinestone, rhinoceros, rhomboid, rhododendron, rhubarb**
ghastly, ghost, ghetto, ghoul
khaki, thyme

exhort, exhaust, exhibit, exhilaration

heir, honor, honest, hour, herb, graham,
    shepherd, posthumous, vehicle, vehement,
    annihilate

(plus the words beginning in *wh* listed in Chapter 13)

Silent k: knack, knapsack, knave, knead, knee, kneel,
    knell, knew, knife, knight, knit, knob, knock,
    knoll, knot, know, knowledge, knuckle, knurl

Silent l: could, should, would, solder

half, behalf, calf, salve, salmon

balk, calk, chalk, stalk, talk, walk, folk, yolk

alms, almond, balm, calm, palm, psalm, qualm

Silent m: mnemonic

Silent n: condemn, damn, hymn, autumn, column,
    solemn

Silent p: pneumatic, pneumonia, psalm, pseudo-, psyche

coup, corps, raspberry, ptomaine, receipt

Silent s: aisle, isle, island, viscount, chassis, corps

Silent t: often, soften, mortgage

fasten, hasten, christen, glisten, listen, moisten

castle, nestle, trestle, wrestle, bristle, gristle,
    thistle, whistle, jostle, bustle, hustle, rustle

Christmas

(also in French-derived words that end in *t:*
ballet, bouquet, etc.)

Silent w: wrack, wraith, wrangle, wrap, wrath, wreak,
    wreath, wreck, wren, wrench, wrest, wrestle,
    wretch, wriggle, wring, wrinkle, wrist, write,
    written, writhe, wrong, wroth, wrought,
    wrung, wry

awry, sword, answer, two

who, whom, whose, whole, whore

Other extraordinary spellings

f sound spelled gh: laugh, enough, rough, slough, tough

(These are the only common words spelled with *gh* representing the *f* sound.)

n sound doubled before ending: **questionnaire, mayonnaise** (in words that don't have a double *n* to begin with)

Silent i: **parliament**

ay pronounced long e: **quay**

oy pronounced long e: **buoy**

w sounded but not spelled: **choir**

Words to Learn

Have someone test you on the above words and list the ones you must memorize.

PART IV

Words Derived from Greek and Latin

15

Regularities in Greek- and Latin-Derived Words

Most of the words in an intelligent person's vocabulary have been taken from Greek or Latin. That's because, until the time of the Renaissance, few English people needed to communicate about anything more than farming, eating, sleeping, and taking part in simple pleasures. When the cultural and social revolution came in—bringing new machines, new ideas, and a completely new way of life—new words had to be invented. Since the writers, printers, and others in charge of explaining and describing were accustomed to communicating in Latin and Greek, they made new words using the Latin and Greek words that most closely described what they meant. And we're still doing that today— for example, in creating **televideo**, *tele-* comes straight from a Greek word that means *far, vide* comes from a Latin verb *videre* that means *to see,* and *-o* is an English add-on to show similarity to words like *audio.*

Most older words are made up entirely of either Latin parts or Greek parts. Some Latin words came to us indirectly through other languages, but we can lump them into this discussion because they follow the spelling rules for Latin- and Greek-derived words.

As we stated briefly in Chapter 4, all Latin- and Greek-derived words begin with roots, to which one or many prefixes and/or suffixes may be added to form longer words:

contemporary = *con* (with) + *tempor* (time) + *ary*
(this word is an adjective)

The spelling of these words is even more closely tied to their sound than is the spelling of native English words. There are fewer rule-breakers, too, though—as in all languages—there are exceptions to the general patterns described below.

The important first step to spelling these words correctly is to say them correctly. If you say *reconize* instead of *recognize,* you'll spell it wrong. If you say *pome* instead of *po-em,* you'll have trouble with it, too. So before you read on, go back and review the five important steps to spelling that we outlined on the first page of Chapter 1.

We've introduced some Greek- and Latin-derived words in previous chapters. You may have noticed that they don't all conform, in spelling pattern, to the two basic native English patterns, the doubling of consonants after a short vowel sound or the use of silent *e* to show a long vowel sound. Let's see what patterns they do follow.

Accented roots

You can usually tell the root of a Latin- or Greek-derived word just by listening to how it's pronounced. Pronounce the following words, then divide them into syllables and place the accent mark after the accented syllable. Can you find the pattern?

reconsidered	appointment	commiserate
division	attractive	militant
corporation	construction	accountant
misinform	innocuous	obscure

Compare the accent in the above words with the accent in some long native American words:

stonecutter	greediness	grandmother
chimneypot	wordfinder	monkeyshines
sodajerk	chamberpot	jazzmobile

Pattern for pronouncing Latin- and Greek-derived words: Unlike native American words, which are usually accented _____, Latin- and Greek-derived words usually accent the _____.
To see if you're correct, check with the chapter summary.

Most of the roots are one syllable, but some are two syllables long. Look at the following two-syllable roots.

> *noxa* (harm): **noxious, obnoxious, innoculate**
> *cumu* (pile up): **cumulative, accumulate**
> *celer* (swift): **accelerate, celerity**
> *fide* (faith): **fidelity**

The accent may be on the _____ syllable of a two-syllable root.

Notice what sometimes happens to the accent when more than one suffix is added to a word:

> **accelerate - acceleration**
> **accumulate - accumulation**
> **admonish - admonition**
> **sequence - consequentially**

Sometimes the accent may even shift into the prefix, to mimic native American pronunciation:

> **infidel   antidote   precinct**

Nonetheless, accent is a helpful guide to locating most roots.

The *schwa*

Look again at this chapter's list that compares native English words with Greek- and Latin-derived words. Did you notice how much stronger is the accent—and how much weaker the unaccented syllables—in Latin- and Greek-derived words? (This is particularly true in Latin-derived words, and less so in Greek-derived ones.) If not, again say both sets of words aloud. Notice that you can hear every vowel in a native English word (*chimneypot, monkeyshines*) —except, perhaps, for the short *e* in an *-er* ending. But in the word **accommodate,** both the first *a* and the second *o* sound like that very short *uh* sound in our native *-er* ending.

Here are some more words that have that distinctive short *uh* sound in the italicized letters. Say them aloud as if you were speaking them to a friend.

ancest*o*r	in*co*mpat*i*ble	vol*u*nteer
impass*a*ble	imper*a*tive	mem*o*rand*u*m
nitrogen*ou*s	rec*i*procity	standard*i*ze
spec*u*lative	*u*nconvent*io*nal	prom*i*nent

As you can see, the sound can be made by *a, e, i, o, u*—and even *ou.* It's this non-native sound, which linguists have named the *schwa,* that causes us all—even the best spellers among us—to occasionally misspell a word. (The *schwa,* a Hebrew word meaning "the sound that isn't heard clearly in unaccented syllables of words," is written as an upside-down e in most dictionary pronunciation guides: ə.)

The *-er* sound is the hardest one in the English language, because it contains the *schwa* sound in combination with the consonant that tends to blur vowel sounds even in accented syllables. Although the most common spelling is *-er,* there are many words spelled *-ir, -ur, -or, -ar,* and a few spelled *-ear, -our.* There's even *were,* which fits into none of these categories.

There is no way to know with your ears how the *schwa* sound is spelled if you listen to ordinary conversation. You must use other aids.

1. Exaggerated enunciation

The best aid we've found is to learn an exaggerated enunciation of these words for spelling purposes: Instead of speaking (or thinking) the *schwa* sound, substitute the short- or long-vowel sound of the letter. (Because we stumbled on this trick back in elementary school, teachers used to think we were "born" spellers.)

EXERCISE 36

Practice substituting the SVS of the italicized letter in the following hard-to-spell words. Once you've said them aloud several dozen times apiece, have someone test you on their spelling.

*a*ccord	rel*a*te	sens*i*tive	comm*i*t	circ*u*mvent
fall*a*cious	frequ*e*nt	citiz*e*n	auton*o*my	murm*u*r
oct*a*ve	an*a*thema	av*i*d	cand*o*r	aug*u*r
caus*a*l	perv*a*de	cred*ible*	prof*e*ss	foc*u*s
blat*a*nt	ferv*e*nt	expl*i*cit	fath*o*m	bog*u*s
cyl*i*nder	def*i*nite	aggr*a*vate	ex*h*ibit	us*a*ge
leg*i*ble	sat*e*llite	elig*i*ble	cand*i*date	vac*u-u*m*
conf*i*dent		cons*i*stent	battal*i*on	app*a*rat*u*s

As you come across other words that you have trouble spelling because of the *schwa* sound, teach yourself a "spelling pronunciation" for each word.

2. Learning prefixes and suffixes

Because *schwas* are contained in the unaccented parts of words that come to us from Greek and Latin, they're usually in a prefix or suffix. If you learn how the common prefixes and suffixes are spelled, you'll eliminate many problems with *schwas*. For instance, the prefix *bene-* (meaning *well*) is always spelled *bene*, never *beni-* or *bena-* or *beno-* or *benu-*. Knowing that, you can always spell the following words correctly:

benefit   beneficial   benevolent   benediction

---

*To learn the spelling of *vacuum*, pronounce it vak-you-um.

Appendix B lists all the common prefixes and suffixes (along with some common roots). You needn't memorize their meanings, but do learn their spellings.

3. Learning demons that confuse

Memorize the following demons that have similar prefixes as well as hard-to-spell *schwa* sounds. (To confuse English even more, we've acquired two *de-* prefixes, the Greek one meaning *binding* and the Latin one meaning *away*. But for spelling purposes we can treat both *de-*'s as one.)

dis-: **disastrous,* discussion, disease, distribute, disappeared, disappoint, discernible, discipline, disparate**

de- and *des-:* **describe, description, desirable, despair, devise, device, desperate, decided, decision, descend, descendant, desert, deceit**

The suffixes *-able* and *-ant* have variant spellings that trick people. Learn these commonly misspelled words.

-ible: **accessible, permissible, discernible, contemptible, indigestible, incredible, irresistible, credible**
(Otherwise, you're most likely correct if you spell the ending *-able*.)

-ent: **dependent, independent, superintendent, competent, confident, consistent, different, efficient, equivalent, excellent, innocent, intelligent, precedent, permanent, persistent, prevalent, prominent, repellent**
(Otherwise, you're most likely correct if you spell the ending *-ant*. The above words also take the *-ence* ending, while other words are usually spelled *-ance*. Don't confuse this ending with *-ment*, which is always spelled with an *e*, not *a*.

---

*This is one of the few English words that drops the *e* of its *er* ending when adding *ous*.

Homonyms:
>   **capital—capitol**
>   **counsel—council**
>   **compliment—complement**
>   **affect—effect**
>   **principal—principle**

Other confusing pairs:
>   **stratagem—strategy**
>   **allege—privilege**
>   **disparate—desperate**
>   **presidents—precedence**
>   **hypocrisy—idiosyncrasy**
>   **repellent—propellant**
>   (*Hypocrisy* comes from *hypocrite,* while *idiosyncrasy* comes from the Greek root *syncran.*)

The best advice we can give for words containing the *schwa* + *r* sound is to look up any word that you're not sure of, and then memorize the word as a spelling demon.

Long and short vowel sounds

As you will recall, long and short vowel sounds in native English words are flagged by the consonant patterns that come after them (SVS = VCCV, LVS = VCV). In Greek- and Latin-derived words, there is no such pattern. Study the following words and see if you can find the pattern for correctly identifying the vowels in italics:

f*e*tal	cond*i*tion	collaborate
contr*o*llable	*a*nimal	m*o*nitor
n*o*tice	per*u*sal	f*u*ngus

Pattern: In Greek- and Latin-derived words, the vowel sound in an accented syllable is nearly always spelled _____

_____, whether followed by one or more consonants.

The pattern is so simple, you may have missed it. It's simply that Greek- and Latin-derived words nearly always spell the vowel sound in an accented syllable exactly the way the vowel sounds!

Doubled letters

Notice above that the word *controllable,* with its doubled *l,* still keeps its long *o* sound, while the word *notice,* with a silent *e* at the end, keeps its short *i* sound. The *e* in notice is there to show that the *c* has an *s* sound (as can be proved if you try to pronounce *notic*), and the doubled *l* doesn't change the sound of the root *rol.*

Now look at the word *collaborate.* Why does it have a doubled *l?* And why the doubled letters in the following words:

accede	dissimilar	reedit	surreptitiou
innate	unnecessary	correspond	nonnative
reenact	accumulate	coordinate	preexist

EXERCISE 37

To find the pattern for doubling letters in Latin- and Greek-derived words, divide the previous words into prefix, root, and suffix. (You may use Appendix B or a dictionary to help you.) Check your answers at the end of the book.
Pattern: In Latin- and Greek-derived words, double letters usually occur when _____.
When two vowel sounds meet, each vowel keeps _____.

There's another common doubling for Latin- and Greek-derived words that's illustrated by the following words. Find the pattern.

occur	occurred	occurrence
prefer	preferred	preferential
demur	demurred	demurrage
appear	apparent	apparition
infer	inferred	inference

Pattern: The letter_____ is usually doubled at the end of an (accented, unaccented) _____ root when preceded by the _____ sound and followed by a _____.
(Notice what happens when the accent shifts out of the root.)
   The *l* sound also sometimes follows this pattern, but it's not dependable:

propel	propellant
council	councillor
counsel	counselor

Assimilation

Study the makeup of the following words with double letters. Notice that something different happens here:

appoint = *ad + point*
affect = *ad + fect*
annex = *ad + nex*
assortment = *ad + sort + ment*
attenuate = *ad + tenu + ate*
allotment = *ad + lot + ment*

What happens to the *d* in the previous words? _____
_____

To understand why it happens, try saying the words as they would have to be pronounced if the letter substitution hadn't been made:

adpoint	adfect	adnex
adsortment	adtenuate	adlotment

This substitution of the first letter of the root, resulting in a doubled letter, is called "assimilation" by linguists. It has occurred in many words where the prefix ends in a consonant and the root begins in a consonant that's hard to say in combination with the prefix. The most-used prefixes of this kind are *ad-*, *com-*, *in-*, *ob-*, and *sub-*.

1. The *d* in *ad-* is often assimilated when followed by *c*, *f*, *g*, *l*, *n*, *p*, *r*, *s*, or *t*. (Before *q* it's changed to *c*: *acquittal*, *acquaint*.)
2. The *m* in *com-* is often assimilated when followed by *l*, *n*, or *r*. It's often changed to *n* when followed by *c*, *d*, *f*, *g*, *j*, *q*, *s*, *t*, or *v*.
3. The *n* in *in-* is often assimilated when followed by *l*, *m*, or *r*.
4. The *b* in *ob-* is often assimilated when followed by *c*, *f*, or *p*.
5. The *b* in *sub-* is often assimilated when followed by *c*, *f*, *g*, *m*, or *p*. (Notice the word *subpoena*, which hasn't been part of English long enough to become assimilated. If it had been, it would have also lost the *o* before the *e*.)

EXERCISE 38

With the help of a dictionary, find at least two examples for each assimilation pattern mentioned above. (Copy the spelling carefully from the dictionary.)

1. ac-   ac-   ac-
    af-   af-   af-
    ag-   ag-   ag-
    al-   al-   al-
    an-   an-   an-
    ap-   ap-   ap-
    ar-   ar-   ar-
    as-   as-   as-
    at-   at-   at-

2.
col-	col-	col-
con-	con-	con-
cor-	cor-	cor-
conc-	conc-	conc-
cond-	cond-	cond-
conf-	conf	conf-
cong-	cong-	cong-
conj-	conj-	conj-
conqu-	conqu-	conqu-
cons-	cons-	cons-
cont-	cont-	cont-
conv-	conv-	conv-

3.
il-	il-	il-
im-	im-	im-
ir-	ir-	ir-

4.
oc-	oc-	oc-
of-	of-	of-
op-	op-	op-

5.
suc-	suc-	suc-
suf-	suf-	suf-
sug-	sug-	sug-
sum-	sum-	sum-
sup-	sup-	sup-

EXERCISE 39

Correct the misspelled words.

affidavit	recuparate	medical
tariff	indispensable	inevitible
resussitate	maintenance	signifigance
surveillance	committee	supprise
colatteral	impromtu	tournamant
comission	necessarily	apparent
hypocriticle	messanger	repellent

Chapter Summary

1. Unlike native American words, which are usually accented at the beginning of the word, Latin- and Greek-derived words usually accent the root.
2. In Greek- and Latin-derived words, the vowel sound in an accented syllable is spelled exactly as it sounds, whether followed by one or more consonants. Unaccented syllables often contain the *schwa* sound, which may be spelled *a, e, i, o, u,* or even *y.*
3. The letter *r* is usually doubled at the end of an accented root that includes a short *u* sound when a suffix beginning with a vowel is added. The letter *l* sometimes follows this pattern.
4. Some doublings occur through assimilation of consonants that don't connect easily in speech.

Words to Learn

Remember to list the words in heavy type that you have trouble spelling, as well as all the words you misspelled in the exercises.

16

The Latin *zh* and *sh* Sounds

Latin-derived words have two special sounds, *zh* and *sh*.

The *zh* sound

The *zh* sound seldom appears in native English words. To spell it, Latin-derived words always use *si*.

    fusion   **diversion**   **incision**   **artesian**   **Asia**

The *sh* sound

Where native English uses the letter cluster *sh* to spell the soft hushing sound, Latin most often uses the letter cluster *ti*. It appears mostly in suffixes, for example *-tion, -tious, -tia,* and *tial.*

    inertia   **motion**   **essential**   **fictitious**   **ini*ti*ation**

Ti is a letter cluster only when followed by another vowel. Notice what happens when *ti* (or one of its sometime substitutes, *ci* or *si*) precedes a consonant:

  par*ti*cularly   **dis*si*milar**   **defi*ci*t**   **par*ti*tion**   **de*ci*sion**

1. Assimilation and the dropped *t*

Notice that the word **excision** is spelled *si,* not *ti.* This is because assimilation takes place. Otherwise the suffix-and-root combination would be a tongue-twister.

    incision = *in + cid + tion*   **tension** = *tens + tion*
    extension = *ex + tend + tion*

There are some roots that end in a short vowel sound followed by *ss*. These words almost always drop the *t* in adding the ending *-tion*. Here are a few examples:

mission = *miss* + *tion*
aggression = *ad* + *gress* + *tion*
concussion = *con* + *cuss* + *tion*
procession = *pro* + *cess* + *tion*
impression = *im* + *press* + *tion*

A good way to remember how to spell these words is to drop the *-tion* ending and substitute an ending that begins with a vowel. You'll have no trouble spelling the root in these words:

aggression	**concussion**	**procession**	**impression**
aggressive	**concussive**	**processive**	**impressive**

In fact, that technique sometimes works for other *-ion* words as well:

extension—extensive
tension—tenseness
action—active

There are some foolers, however, for example:

intention—intensive

That's because the root (meaning *to stretch*) can be spelled *tens* or *tent*.

Another demon to learn is:

omit—omission

(The letter *t* can't be pronounced before *-tion*. In this case they're both changed instead of one being dropped.)

2. *ci* spelling

A few words spell the *ti* sound *ci*. On the whole, this is due to assimilation in which the *t* is dropped. But a few words come from Latin roots:

crux—crucial
species—special
society—social
coerce—coercion

Since there are so few commonly used words that spell the *ti* sound *ci,* memorize the ones you have trouble with:

verbs	*adjectives*	*nouns*
appreciate	ancient	acacia
associate	artificial	
	atrocious	academician
depreciate	audacious	beautician
emaciate	auspicious	clinician
	avaricious	coercion
excruciate	beneficial	electrician
glaciate	capacious	fiduciary
	capricious	logician
	commerical	magician
	crucial	mathematician
	delicious	mortician
	efficacious	musician
	facial	obstetrician
	fallacious	paramecium
	ferocious	patrician
	financial	pediatrician
	glacial	physician

verbs	*adjectives*	*nouns*
	gracious	politician
	judicial	statistician
	judicious	species
	loquacious	suspicion
	malicious	technician
	mendacious	
	meretricious	
	official	
	officious	
	pernicious	
	perspicacious	
	precious	
	precocious	
	prejudicial	
	provincial	
	racial	
	rapacious	
	sacrificial	
	sagacious	
	salacious	
	sociable	
	social	
	spacious	
	special	
	specious	
	superficial	
	suspicious	
	tenacious	
	ungracious	
	vicious	
	vivacious	
	voracious	

EXERCISE 40

To shorten the above list, for every possible word, find

another word with the same root that will help you remember to spell the word *ci* instead of *ti*. (Our selections are listed in the answer section at the end of the book.)

We can sum up our study of *-ti, -si,* and *-ci* with a general rule once you've learned the exceptions noted above. Pattern: the *sh* sound in Latin-derived word endings is spelled *-ti,* except in the following general instances: If the root word ends in *-ss* or soft *c,* the *t* is usually dropped; and if the root word ends in *s,* the *t* is usually changed to *s.*

3. *sh* spelled *ce*

There are only four commonly used words in which the sound *sh* is spelled *ce.* They're all derived from Latin. Memorize their spelling.

curvaceous   crustacean   herbaceous   ocean

These words were also mentioned in Chapter 13. It might be wise to review that chapter's discussion of the *sh* sound now.

4. The accent shift

You may have noticed that each example word in this chapter is accented in the syllable immediately preceding the *sh* sound. Notice how the accent has shifted, in many cases, right out of the root word:

affectation   convolution   perdition

This accent shift is true for most Latin-derived words. It's a matter of conversational convenience: since the *sh* sound takes time to form, accenting the previous syllable gives the speaker just the tiny pause that's needed for the lips to form *sh.*

5. The *k* + *sh* sound

Latin-derived words, and a few others that have come from other languages, sometimes combine the *k* sound with an *sh* sound. In Great Britain, many of these words spell the *ksh* combination with an *x* (for example, the U.S. *connection* is spelled *connexion* in Great Britain). But in the United States, we've changed the spelling of most of those words to conform to regular spelling patterns. The only common words that still use the *x* spelling in the United States are:

anxious   noxious   crucifixion

(For other irregular *sh* spellings, see Chapter 13.)

EXERCISE 41

Correct the incorrectly spelled words.

anxious	socialization
financial	disimilar
imaginitive	ajust
immitation	sufficient
connexion	occurrence
repetitious	supplamental
repetetive	succession
pronounciation	supressing
organisation	colateral
influencial	comission
discription	immediatly
inactsion	affidavit
pernitious	strategy
suspicion	hypocrisy

Chapter Summary

1. In Latin-derived words, the sound *zh* is always spelled *si.*

2. In Latin-derived words, the sound *sh* is spelled *ti* except that if the root word ends in -*ss* or a soft -*c,* the *t* is usually dropped; and if the root word ends in -*s,* the *t* is usually changed to *s.*

Words to Learn

List the heavy-type words you can't spell, as well as the words misspelled in the exercises.

17

Special Greek-Derived Spellings:
ph, y, ch (and *rh, mn, pn,* and *ps*)

The Greek alphabet has certain peculiarities which have been carried over into English word borrowings.

1. The *f* sound is spelled *ph*

Keep in mind that many commonly used words in this category either begin with *ph* or are derived from words that begin with *ph*. The following list includes many words that are fun to use, once you can spell them:

phalanx	amphibian	blaspheme
phallic	emphatic	ephemeral
phantasm	lymph	euphoria
phantom	morphology	nephritis
pharmacy	prophet	schizophrenia
pharynx	sophisticated	symphony
phase	typhoon	alpha
pheasant	amorphous	amphitheater
phlegm	apostrophe	asphalt
phaeton	atrophy	graph
phobia	blasphemy	camphor
phoenix	catastrophe	cellophane
phone	chlorophyll	cipher
phosphate	diaphragm	dolphin
phosphorus	elephant	emphasis
photo	euphemism	gopher
phrase	hyphen	metaphor
physical	neophyte	orphan

philanthropy	pamphlet	paraphernalia
philharmonic	seraphim	prophylactic
philosophy	triumph	trophy
phenomenon	typhoid	
phantasmagoria	phrenetic	phlegmatic

In learning *ph* words, look for the Greek prefix *philo* (meaning *love of*), the root *graph* (meaning *writing*), the suffix *phobia* (meaning *fear of*), and other common Greek roots.

2. The long *i* and short *i* sounds are often spelled y

Study the above list of *ph* words to see how commonly *y* is substituted for both short *i* and long *i*. However, the substitution isn't always made. Notice in Appendix B how many Greek suffixes (and some prefixes as well) contain the letter *i*.

Below are some of the most frequently used words that are spelled with *y*.

a. Long *i* sound

cycle	hybrid	hydrant	hydrogen
hygiene	hyphen	python	pylon
type	stylus	tyrant	typhus

In addition the prefixes *psycho-*, *pyro-*, *typo-*, *hydro-*, *hypo-*, and *hyper-*, and the root *cyclo-* (as in *encyclopedia*) are all spelled with *y*.

b. Short *i* sound

acronym	amethyst	antonym	bicycle
abyss	calypso	cataclysm	onyx
crypt	crystal	cylinder	cymbal
cynic	cyst	dysentary	glycerin
gym	gyp	gypsum	gypsy

hypnotize	hypocrite	idiosyncracy	idyllic
larynx	lymph	lynch	lynx
lyric	myriad	mystic	myth
nymph	physics	polygamy	pygmy
pyramid	rhythm	sycamore	syllable
sylvan	symbol	symmetry	sympathy
symphony	symptom	synagogue	syphilis
syringe	syrup	system	tryst
typical	tyranny		

In addition, the prefixes *dys-, sym-,* and *syn-,* and the root *hypno-* are popular in Greek-derived words.

(Notice that some of the above words are also in the *ph* spelling list.)

3. The sound *k* Is usually spelled *ch*

This Greek spelling, *ch* or *k,* occurs mostly in front of a vowel. We've already seen the spelling in words with the root *psycho.* Other popular roots are *schizo, synchro, schol* (as in **scholar**), *chrono* (as in **chronology**), *archi* (as in **architect, oligarchy,** and **anarchist**). Here are some other words that are fun to use, and that many people avoid writing simply because they're unsure of the spelling.

ache	echo	stomach	technique
archaic	bronchitis	chaos	character
chasm	chemical	chlorine	chiropractor
chorus	christen	chrome	chrysalis
dichotomy	inchoate	mechanic	orchestra
alchemy	anchor	archetype	melancholy
archive	chameleon	chimera	chromatic
ocher	leprechaun	orchid	harpsichord
lichen	parochial	school	sepulcher
scheme	schedule	schooner	epoch
masochist	pachyderm		

4. Some silent letters are of Greek origin

One favorite Greek spelling that has been borrowed by English is to spell some words *rh* for *r*. (The sound was actually an *r* + *h* sound in Greek, but we don't use it in English.) Most of the common *rh* words have been listed in Chapter 14.

A few Greek words beginning in *mn, pn, ps,* and *pt* have also been borrowed. It pays to look up these words in a good pronouncing dictionary to see how they're pronounced in English. Here are a few words to start you off:

mnemonic   **pneumatic**   **psoriasis**   **pterodactyl**

5. Assimilation

Assimilation rarely occurs in Greek-derived words, since most prefixes end in a vowel. The main exception is the prefix *syn-*, which means *together* or *at the same time.* When it's added to roots beginning with *l* or *m*, assimilation usually occurs:

syn + *log* + *ism* = **syllogism**
syn + *laba* = **syllable**
syn + *metron* = **symmetry**

When it's added to roots beginning with *b* or *p*, the *n* changes to *m:*

syn + *pathy* = **sympathy**
syn + *bios* + *is* = **symbiosis**

EXERCISE 42

Correct the incorrectly spelled words and tell whether the roots are derived from Latin or Greek.

symbol

criticism

mystification

cystern

conception

rhomboyd

substanciate

neumatic

enmity

phisician

analize

fanomenon

inphluential

scedule

sophomoric

cilinder

psychology

publicly

ninth

naphtha

sacrifice

ecstasy

syncerely

diaphragm

Chapter Summary

1. In Greek-derived words, the *f* sound is spelled *ph*, the long *i* and short *i* sounds are often spelled *y*, and the sound *k* is usually spelled *ch*. In addition, the letter clusters *rh, mn, pn, ps,* and *pt* are of Greek origin.
2. Assimilation rarely occurs in Greek-derived words, except in connection with the prefix *syn-*.

Words to Learn

Have someone test your spelling of the words in this chapter in heavy type and add your demons here along with words you misspelled in Exercise 42.

PART V

Invasion Words

18

Patterns in Invasion Words

Up until now, the primary rule of English spelling—each sound is represented by a letter unless there's a good reason—has held up. For native English and Greek- and Latin-derived words, more than 98 percent can be said to be regular. That is, they're spelled the way they sound.

But throughout our discussion of various sounds, we've also scattered groups of words that don't follow the rules: for instance, the words in Chapter 8 that spell the *z* sound *ss*. These are primarily Invasion words. They have come to us from all the languages with which English-speaking people have had contact, going as far back as the tenth century and earlier. Happily, these words make up only from 10 to 15 percent of the language—and even with these words, we can find some generalizations that apply.

Homonyms

When many of these words invaded English, they bumped smack up against other words that sounded so similar, the difference in meaning could only be deciphered in context. The authors of our written communication devised a solution that the spoken language couldn't offer: they spelled these new words with alternate vowel sounds. That's how most of the homonyms in our language were born.

| sale—sail | bore—boar | forth—fourth |
| hole—whole | steel—steal | I'll—isle—aisle |

These short words trip up many good spellers. The best way to learn to spell each variant correctly is to memorize each spelling *in association with* the word's meaning, actually picturing the meaning in your mind as you study the word. Throughout the book, we've tried to list every homonym—and near-homonym—that is frequently misspelled.

Doubled consonants

For the most part, the consonants in Invasion words are pronounced exactly as in native English words. Since they're spelled the way they sound, they rarely give any trouble. But there's a small group of two-syllable verbs from the romance languages—particularly French—that retain their native accent on the second syllable instead of shifting it to the first syllable. Here are a few examples:

occur	occurring	occurred	occurrence
allot	allotting	allotted	allotment
prefer	preferring	preferred	preference
corral	corralling	corralled	corrals

What happens to the spelling when we add endings that begin with a vowel? _____

What happens when the accent shifts into the first syllable?

_____

This doubling of the final consonant also occurs in a few native English verbs. See if you can find a pattern for when to double and when not to, by examining each list below. (We've added *-ing,* but the same spelling holds true if you add any ending beginning with a vowel.)

accent on *1st syllable*	*accent on second syllable*		
	2nd syll = SVS	*2nd syll = SVS*	*2nd syll = LVS*
gallop*(ing)*	occur*(ring)*	predict*(ing)*	devise*(ing)*
ballot*(ing)*	allot*(ting)*	lament*(ing)*	console*(ing)*
barrel*(ing)*	corral*(ling)*	insert*(ing)*	prevail*(ing)*
proffer*(ing)*	prefer*(ring)*	remark*(ing)*	retire*(ing)*

accent on 1st syllable	accent on second syllable		
	2nd syll = SVS	2nd syll = SVS	2nd syll = LVS
armor*(ing)*	**defer***(ring)*	**collect***(ing)*	**inquire̸***(ing)*
target*(ing)*	**forget***(ting)*	**corrupt***(ing)*	**refute̸***(ing)*
tunnel*(ing)*	**rebel***(ling)*	**exist***(ing)*	**unpeel***(ing)*
conjure̸*(ing)*	**begin***(ning)*	**connect***(ing)*	**disappear***(ing)*
benefit*(ing)*	**transfer***(ring)*	**embalm***(ing)*	**carouse̸***(ing)*

Pattern for doubling the last letter when adding endings to words accented on the final syllable: Double the final consonant if needed, so that the spelling follows the pattern SVS = ____ and LVS = ____.

Notice that the two-consonant pattern acts as a pronunciation guide for readers: English readers, seeing a two-consonant grouping after the first syllable of a word, learn to put the accent on that syllable. If they see the two-consonant pattern suddenly in the last syllable of the root (even if there's also a two-consonant pattern in the first syllable), they know that this is usually the syllable to accent. Watch for this clue as you read for pleasure.

When a verb changes the spelling of its root to make its adjective form, the doubling pattern of the root word is often kept. This sometimes results in a seeming exception to the pattern we've observed.

appear—apparent
excel—excellent

EXERCISE 43

Add the indicated suffix to the following words. Check your spelling with the answer section in the back of the book.

arrive (al)	benefit (ed)
procure (ment)	stretch (ing)
schedule (ed)	reflect (ive)

reflex (ive)

consider (ate)

rebel (ed)

infer (ence)

transfer (ing)

indemn (ity)

corrode (ing)

revel (ry)

confuse (ion)

incur (ed)

oblige (ing)

corrupt (ed)

standard (ize)

conform (ed)

alter (ing)

retain (ed)

contain (ment)

Chapter Summary

1. The influx of words from other languages has created most of the homonyms in English.
2. Words from other languages often are accented on the last syllable instead of the first.
3. When adding endings to words accented on the final syllable, double the final consonant if needed, so that the spelling follows the pattern SVS = VCCV and LVS = VCV.

Words to Learn

List the heavy-type words you can't spell, as well as the words misspelled in the exercises.

19

Irregular Spellings
of Vowel Sounds

Back in Chapter 2 we studied the native English spellings of the vowel sounds. We saw that the long vowel sounds sound exactly the same as their letter names except for *u* (whose letter name, *yu,* is used only for some words and in some regions of America):

a as in **cake**
e as in **she** (often doubled, as in **weep**)
i as in **wipe**
o as in **rode**
u as in **fume**

But you've probably noticed by now that each of the above sounds is also commonly spelled at least one other way (in addition to the spellings that occur when we add the helping letter *e* discussed in Chapter 7). Here are some of the ways.

a:	**cake**	**bait**	**rein**	
e:	**she**	**beet**	**cheap**	
i:	**bike**	**fight**	**trial**	**fry**
o:	**cope**	**whoa**	**mow**	
u:	**rude**	**lewd**	**feud**	**due**	**boot**

Many of these alternate spellings begin to make sense (even though they don't make our spelling task any easier) once we understand that all of our long vowel sounds—except *e* and sometimes *u*—are really *diphthongs.* That's a Greek-derived word composed of *di* meaning *two* and *phthongos* (*ph* is pronounced *f*) meaning *sounds*. In a diphthong, the first sound is the one that's accented—but unless you also briefly add the second sound, the vowel doesn't sound quite right.

It'll help your spelling if you train your ear to hear the separate sounds that make up most long vowel sounds. Practice the following exercise several times.

EXERCISE 44

Say each nonsense word in the last column several times, faster and faster, until you can hear the long vowel sound (and the real word) created by sliding one short vowel sound into the next. (See the answer section if you're unsure of the words created)

LVS	Makeup	Real word	Nonsense word
a	SVS *e* + SVS *i*	**their**	*ke + il*
i	ah + SVS *i*	**vial**	*trah + il*
o	LVS *o* + SVS *oo*	**goat**	*ko + oot*
u	SVS *i* + SVS *oo*	**few**	*fi + oodal*

Because some of the first transcribers of our written language attempted to mimic the double sound of new diphthongs as they came into our language through Invasion words, we have several alternate spellings for these sounds. *Trial* was spelled that way because it sounded to the first spellers like *tri-* + *al*. *Fail* was spelled that way because it sounded like *fa* (as in *family*) + *il*. *Hear* was spelled that way because it sounded like *he* + *a* (as in the word *a*) + *r*.

One pattern early transcribers found that really makes for problem spelling today was to add an *a* after a long vowel sound to signify LVS.

throat   liable   steal

Unfortunately, it wasn't done with any dependable regularity.

Another development that led to irregular spellings was the fashionable practice of attempting to trace even pure old native English words to what the transcribers guessed were their Latin and Greek roots. Words with perfectly good English spellings were changed to conform to these often incorrect roots. *Dette* became *debt* to conform to the Latin word *debitum*. The spelling of *receit* was changed to *receipt* because of false tracing to the Latin *receptum*.

These strange spellings are mostly in words we all learned long ago to spell—or never quite learned. If you memorize the following words in the groups into which we've divided them, you'll find them easier to remember.

Alternate spellings of long *a* sound

The most frequent alternate spelling of the long *a* sound is the letter *a* with an *i* added to represent that short *i* sound in the diphthong:

frail	**main**	**gaily**	**hair**
waiver	**sustain**	**repair**	**liaison** (*li + ai + son*)

This alternate spelling occurs mostly before *l* and *r,* because the short *i* sound is most evident before *l* and *r:*

fail	**quail**	**prevail**
hair	**prairie**	**repair**

Notice that the long *a* sound changes slightly in front of the *r* sound. That's true of several vowel sounds.

Below are the most common exceptions to the *ai + l* pattern.

ale	**gale**	**sale**	**impale**
alias	**hale**	**scale**	**regale**
alien	**kale**	**shale**	**salient**
azalea	**pale**	**whale**	**saline**

Many exceptions to the *ai* + *r* pattern are homonyms:

fair—fare	pair—pear
stair—stare	air—heir
bare—bear	they're—there—their
ware—wear	theirs—there's

and near-homonyms:

vary—very   fairy—ferry

In addition, two-syllable words ending in long *a* + *n* are usually spelled *-ain*. Some examples are **explain, refrain,** and **remain.** But **membrane** and **inane** are exceptions.

Homonyms with long *a* sound

Many *ai* words were spelled that way by early transcribers because there already were words in the language that sounded the same. Notice how many other homonyms fall into the *a* and *ai* categories. (Can you add to the following list?) Study these words, making certain that you know what definition goes with which spelling. (Particularly study the third column, in which the alternate spelling *ei* is introduced. Compare this spelling with the homonym's makeup as described in the previous chart.)

plane—plain	mane—main	faint—feint
ale—ail	made—maid	rain—rein—reign
lane—lain	gate—gait	wait—weight
male—mail	bate—bait	vain—vein
sale—sail	hale—hail	vale—veil
pale—pail	whale—wail	nay—neigh
waste—waist	pane—pain	ate—eight
maze—maize	tale—tail	slay—sleigh
wave—waive	raze—raise	way—weigh
brays—braise	prays—praise	strait—straight
		aid—aide

Most words that end in *-ay* keep the *y* when an ending is added. The major exceptions are:

lay—laid   **pay—paid**   **say—said**

Irregular spellings of long a sound

There are some words in which the spelling of the long *a* sound is quite irregular. They must be memorized:

a = *ae:* **aerial**
a = *au:* **gauge**
a = *ai(gh):* **straight**
a = *ai(g):* **arraign, campaign, champaign**
a = *ea:* **break, great, steak**
　　　　bear, pear, tear, wear, swear
a = *ei:* **beige, feint, heinous, rein, reindeer, skein, veil, vein**
　　　　heir, their, theirs
a = *ey:* **convey, grey** (also **gray**), **obey, prey, purvey, survey, they, whey**
a = *ei(g):* **deign, feign, reign**
a = *ei(gh):* **eight, freight, neigh, sleigh, weigh, weight**
a = *e:* **there, where, ere, bolero**
　　　In addition, *e* is the most common romance language way of spelling the long *a* sound, and most recent imports from those languages keep this spelling:
　　　allegro, andante, cafe, carburetor, crepe, fete, finale, forte, mesa, suede
a = *ee:* **entree, matinee, melee, negligee**

If the word isn't singled out above, and you're not sure of its spelling, you'll most likely be correct if you spell the long *a* sound *a*.

Alternate spellings of long e sound

More than 90 percent of all words with the long *e* sound spell it simply *e*. Another large group, consisting of every multi-syllable word ending in the long *e* sound, spells this final ending *y*, with the exceptions noted below under *ee* and *ie*. (Some linguists say this *y* really represents a short *i* sound.)

any   visionary   democracy   oligarchy

Of the less than 10 percent of words left that contain this most popular vowel sound in English, the most likely spelling is *ee* or *ea*. Most of the one-syllable words (or words derived from them) that fall into this category stem from early English. Here are some examples:

meek	**free**	**speech**	**street**
wheat	**meal**	**weave**	**ease**

We won't list all these one-syllable *ea* and *ee* words but suggest that if you're unsure of the spelling of any one-syllable words containing the long *e* sound, you look them up in a dictionary.

We *will* list the major two-syllable words (that aren't derived from one-syllable words) that contain the spelling *ea* or *ee,* since there are relatively few of them. (Cross out the words you already know how to spell.)

verbs		*nouns*		*other*
ea:				
anneal	impeach	beacon	feature	beneath
appeal	increase	beagle	heathen	deceased
appease	release	beaker	malfeasance	easy
bequeath	reason	beaver	measles	feasible
bereave	repeal	cleavage	ordeal	meager
conceal	repeat	colleague	peacock	piecemeal
congeal	retreat	creature	streamer	queasy

verbs		nouns		other
decrease	reveal	deacon	treason	squeamish
defeat	appear	demeanor	treatise	weary
demean		disease	treatment	
displease		eagle	treaty	
entreat		easel	upheaval	
			weasel	

verbs		nouns		other

ee:

verbs		nouns		other
agree	absentee	esteem	nominee	between
beseech	addressee	feeble	pedigree	discreet
careen	amputee	filigree	perigee	eerie
decree	apogee	fricasee	refugee	genteel
proceed	beetle	grandee	repartee	indeed
redeem	canteen	guarantee	rupee	peevish
referee	chickadee	jubilee	settee	unseemly
succeed	degree	levee	squeegee	
teeter	devotee	marquee	steeple	
wheedle	dungaree	needle	tepee	
		veneer	trustee	

Notice how many of the above words *end* in *ee*. Most of them are French imports in which the *ee* was originally pronounced with a long *a* sound.

In addition, the long *e* sound is spelled *ee* in the ending *-eer* that is tacked onto a number of words such as:

auctioneer   engineer   racketeer

But memorize:

brigadier	**cavalier**	**chandelier**
chiffonier	**financier**	**frontier**
grenadier	**vizier**	

and the one-syllable variant words: **pier, tier**

A few native English words spell the ending long *e* sound *ey*. Notice that the *y* is either kept or changed to *i* and the first *e* dropped, when endings beginning with vowels are added. Otherwise, there'd be the problem of three vowels in a row. (Unfortunately, some words prefer one pattern and other words the other pattern.)

key—keyed
honey—honeyed
money—monied

The English long vowel *e* sounds the same as the romance language LVS *i,* and in some Invasion words the spelling *i* is kept for this sound—for instance, in the words *police* and *petite.* The spelling *i* also appears in some imported endings, notably *-ine, -ise, -iste* (*figurine, chemise, artiste,* etc.), and in many Latin- and Greek-derived endings, although when said quickly the long *e* sound often shortens to sound like the consonant *y* (the sound *yuh*):

ingen*i*ous   rebell*i*on

Study these common words in which the long *e* sound is spelled *i.*

antique	fatigue	fiasco	lien	machine
critique	intrigue	kilo	lira	souvenir
oblique	prestige	casino	diva	finale
technique	mobile	trio	viola	regime
clique	chenille	mosquito	yogi	naive
unique	paprika	maraschino	ski	elite
pique	caprice		timpani	batiste
piquant	motif	liaison	nisei	artiste

Homonyms with long *e* sound

A number of short words are *ee—ea* homonyms, among them:

beat—beet	cheap—cheep	creak—creek
feat—feet	heal—heel	leak—leek
meat—meet	peal—peel	peak—peek
seam—seem	team—teem	weak—week
sea—see	read—reed	real—reel

In addition memorize:

peace—piece	need—knead
freeze—frieze	mean—mien

Irregular spellings of long e sound

e = *ei:* ceiling, conceit, conceive, deceive, either,
inveigle,* leisure, neither, perceive, receive,
seize, sheik, weird

(Five of the above words come through Old
French and contain the root *ceive,* meaning
to take. Also notice that "*i* before *e* except
after *c*" isn't always true.)

e = *ei(p):* receipt

e = *eo:* people

e = *ie:* achieve, believe, besiege, brassiere, brief, chief,
coterie, fief, field, fiend, fierce, frieze,
grieve, grievous, hygiene, liege, mien, niece,
piece, pierce, priest, relieve, reprieve,
retrieve, reverie, shield, shriek, siege, thief,
wield, yield

(See also *-ier* ending already discussed.)

e = *oe:* amoeba, phoebe, phoenix, subpoena

(This is a transliteration of a Greek spelling.)

Once you've learned all the words mentioned above, you
won't go far wrong if you spell every other long *e* sound with
an *e*.

---

*This word can be pronounced *in-vay' -guhl* or *in-vee' -guhl.*

The long *i* sound and the ending *y*

The long *i* sound has the most regular spelling of the long vowel sounds. Most words spell the sound *i* if it's in the middle of a word, with a silent *e* added at the end if needed to make the word conform to the pattern we studied back in Chapter 7. If the long *i* sound comes at the end of a word, it's spelled *y*—for a logical reason.

The first transcribers were afraid that the little *i*, with its simple one-stroke makeup, would be overlooked by the rapid reader. So in the middle of a word they added a dot above it to highlight it—and at the end of a word they added a downward flourish to the final upward stroke. When the ending beginning with *i* (*-ing*) had to be added to words, the little *i* was again written with a flourish to distinguish it from the next *i*:

try   trying   tried   trial

That fancy *i* eventually got to look just like a *y*—which is why the letter *y* represents both the consonant we've already discussed, and the letter *i* at the end of a word or before *-ing*.

Pattern: We don't "drop the y *and add* i*" when putting endings on words, but instead change the* i *to* y *for final endings and before the letter* i.

This point helps us understand why the spelling *ai* (for long *a*) changes to *ay* in some cases but not in others. Take the words *pay* and *stay* and see how each word would look if the *ai* were kept throughout all the various derivatives:

+ *ed* = *paied*   + *ing* = *paiing*   + *able* = *paiable*
+ *ed* = *staied*   + *ing* = *staiing*   + *able* = *staiable*

Notice that this would create a situation in which there were *three vowels in a row*—and no native English word (and very few nonnative ones) has three vowels in a row. In some cases (*paid,* for example), one of the vowels was dropped; in others, (*stayable,* for example), the *i* was changed to its *y* spelling. It's these diphthong-derived spellings that end in the letter *i* that have created most of the irregular verb spellings we struggled over in school.

We can sum up our discussion with the following rule: *Pattern: If the spelling* ai, ei, oi, ui, *or* i *comes at the end of a word, the* i *is changed to* y. Keep in mind that this is the variant spelling of *i,* and not the consonant *y,* and many of your spelling problems will disappear.

The *ie* ending: A variant of *y*

A few common words don't change the *i* to *y,* but add a silent *e* instead to show the LVS. Memorize them.

die   **fie**   **hie**   **lie**   **magpie**   **pie**   **tie**   **vie**

These words keep the *ie* ending even as part of longer words (*untie*) but most of them change regularly before endings (*vying, vied*).

Demon to learn: **fire—fiery**

The Greek letter *y* for the long *i* sound

We've already discussed the fact that the Greeks used the letter *y* for *i* in many places, and that these spellings have been retained in English. (This may be what led later transcribers to make the *i-y* end-of-word substitution.) Here are the most common words that include *y* for the long *i* sound.

asylum	**pylon**	**tycoon**
byte	**python**	**typhoid**
dryad	**thyme**	**typhoon**
enzyme	**rhyme**	**tyrant**
lyceum	**stylus**	**tyro**
lyre	**style**	**scythe**

A number of familiar words all come from the same Greek roots. Here are the roots and some of the words derived from them.

cy: **cyanide, cybernetics, cynosure, cypress** (etc.)
cyclo: **bicycle, cycle, cyclone, encyclopedia**
dy: **dynamo, dynamite, dynamic, dynasty** (etc.)
gyr: **gyrate, gyroscope** (etc.)
hy: **hyacinth, hybrid, hyphen, hygiene**
hydro: **hydrochloric, hydrolics, hydrant** (etc.)
hyper: **hyperbola, hypercritical, hypothesis**
pyro: **pyre, pyrite, pyromania, pyrotechnics**
psyche: **psychic, psychiatry, psychology** (etc.)
typo: **type, typify, typographic**

The following Greek endings should be learned, too:

type: **archetype, prototype** (etc.)
lyte: **electrolyte, proselyte**
phyte: **neophyte**

Homonyms with long *i* sound

A few of the strange spellings of the long *i* sound have been created because of homonyms. Memorize the difference between these twins:

mite—might	**rite—right**	**site—sight**
by—buy—bye	**hi—high**	**slight—sleight**
I'll—aisle—isle	**libel—liable**	**stile—style**
I—eye	**die—dye**	**lie—lye**

(Notice that the first *lie* has two meanings, to tell a falsehood and to put oneself parallel to the floor—but that transcribers ran out of ways to spell the vowel sound.)

Irregular spellings of long *i* sound

i = ai(s): **aisle**
i = ay: **bayou, cayenne, kayak**

i = *ei:* **feisty, seismic, stein, poltergeist, kaleidoscope**
i = *ei(gh):* **height, sleight**
i = *ey:* **geyser, eye**
i = *i(gh):* **blight, bright, delight, fight, fright, knight,**
light, might, night, plight, right, sight,
slight, tight
(The above very old English words
originally pronounced the *gh* sound very
much as *ch* is pronounced in German,
with a sound halfway between *h* and *k*.)
high, sigh, thigh
i = *oy:* **coyote**
i = *uy:* **buy, guy**
i = *y in the*
middle of a word: **dye, lye, rye, analyze, paralyze**
(Notice **analysis, paralytic,** etc.— remember the rule
that the whole little word is included in the longer
word.)

Alternate spellings of the long *o* sound

The long *o* sound is spelled *o* nearly 95 percent of the time.
The next most popular spelling is *oa*. Here are most of the
commonly used *oa* words. Learn them and the few variants
listed below and you'll have no trouble with this sound.

The long *o* sound spelled *oa*

verbs	*nouns*		*verb and noun*		*other*
approach	**boar**	**oak**	**board**	**load**	**hoary**
bloat	**boat**	**oar**	**boast**	**loaf**	**loath**
coax	**coal**	**oat**	**broach**	**moan**	
encroach	**coat**	**oath**	**cloak**	**roar**	
gloat	**cocoa**	**roach**	**coast**	**roast**	
poach	**foal**	**road**	**coach**	**soap**	
reload	**goat**	**roan**	**float**	**toast**	
reproach	**hoax**	**shoal**	**foam**		

verbs		nouns	verb and noun	other
roam	loam	throat	goad	
soak	goal	toad	groan	
soar	loan	moat		

Notice how many of the above words refer to animals. Have someone test you and cross out the words you already know how to spell. Then memorize the few that are left.

The long *o* sound, like most vowel sounds, changes before the sound *r*. But notice that it changes more than most sounds do, becoming almost exactly like the sound *aw*. We'll look at it again when we get to *aw* in the next chapter.

Irregular spellings of long *o* sound

The following spelling variations of the long *o* sound come from French:

>*o = au:* **chauffeur, hauteur, restaurant, gauche, mauve**
>*o = eau:* **beau, bureau, plateau, tableau, trousseau**

The rest come from various languages:

>*o = ew:* **sew** (the only word having this substitution)
>*o = oh:* **oh, ohm**
>*o = oo:* **brooch, door, floor**
>*o = ou:* **boulder, cantaloupe, mould, poultice, poultry, soul**
>*o = ou(gh):* **although, dough, though, borough, furlough, thorough**

Homonyms with long *o* sound

lone—loan	rode—road	lode—load
so—sew	bow—beau	oh—owe
soul—sole	mold—mould	shone—shown

Alternate spellings of the long *u* sound

Many linguists define the long *u* sound as the *u* we hear in the word *few* and assign another category to the long *u* sound that appears in words like *food*. However, the long *u* sound in words like *few* is really a diphthong consisting of the short vowel sound *i* (or, as some linguists define it, the consonant *y*) + the long *u* sound. To hear the diphthong clearly, say these words over and over:

universal	**accumulate**	**feud**	**venture**
communal	**virtual**	**endure**	**manual**

Most short *i* + long *u* (*yu*) sound words are spelled with *u*, but *oo* sound words can be spelled with either *u* or *oo*. (If the word is derived from Latin or Greek it is always spelled *u* and never *oo*.)

Any difference that may have once existed between the *u* sound in *food* and the *u* sound in *accrue* has largely disappeared from American speech. The sound distinction between *yu* and *oo* is still used to clarify between the following near-homonyms:

feud—food   cue—coo   due—do

But several variant spellings are introduced for the following homonyms:

blue—blew	**choo—chew**	**flu—flew**
yew—you	**dual—duel**	**threw—through**
two—to—too	**new—knew—gnu**	

A word that ends with *u* for both sound and spelling adds a silent *e*:

revenue   pursue   imbue

That silent *e* is kept even when the common English endings are added—but in a few cases it changes to silent *i*:

suit   pursuit

We'll list most of the common *yu* sound words that aren't spelled simply with *u,* and *oo* sound words that aren't spelled with either *u* or *oo.* Memorize these irregular spellings.

Variant patterns: *yu* sound words

In some regions of the country, the *y* is dropped in some of these words.

yu = *eau:* **beauty**
yu = *eu:* **amateur, deuce, feud, grandeur, neurotic, neuter, neutral, neutron, pneumatic, pneumonia, therapeutic**
eulogy, eunuch, euphemism, euphoria
yu = *ew:* **dew, ewe, few, hew, knew, mew, new, news, newt, pew, skewer, stew, whew**
curfew, mildew, nephew, sinew
yu = *ieu:* **adieu**
yu = *iew:* **view** (and its derivatives)
yu = *ui:* **nuisance**

Variant patterns: *oo* sound words

oo = *eu:* **sleuth, maneuver, rheumatism, pseudo**
oo = *ew:* **blew, brew, chew, drew, flew, grew, jewel, lewd, sewer, screw, shrewd, slew, strew, threw, yew**
oo = *ieu:* **lieu, lieutenant**
oo = *o:* **approve, do, lose, move, movie, prove, to, tomb, two, who, whom, whose, womb**
oo = *oe:* **canoe, shoe**

oo = ou: acoustic, bayou, bouquet,* boulevard,
            caribou, cougar, coulee, coupon, croup,
            goulash, group, insouciance, louver,
            nougat, rouge, roulette, route, routine,
            soup, souvenir, troubador, troupe,
            trousseau, uncouth, wound, youth
oo = ou(gh): through
oo = ue: accrue, blue, clue, construe, flue, fondue,
            glue, gruesome, rue, Tuesday, true
oo = ui: bruise, cruise, fruit, juice, sluice, suit, pursuit

Demons among the short vowel sounds

The short vowel sounds are quite regular in their spellings.
We'll list only those words that have irregular spellings, are
most commonly misspelled, and haven't been treated else-
where in the book.

short a: **plaid**
short e: **orange, again, against, aesthetic, said, says,
            heifer, cleanse, jeopardy, leopard, friend,
            bury**
            Many of the following words were once
            pronounced with a long *a* sound. The
            spelling has survived the change in
            pronunciation:
            **bread, breadth, breast, breath, cleanly,
            dead, deaf, dealt, death, dread, endeavor,
            feather, head, health, heather, heaven,
            heavy, instead, jealous, lead, leapt, leather,
            leaven, meadow, meant, measure, peasant,
            pleasant, read, ready, realm, spread, stead,
            stealth, sweat, thread, threat, treachery,
            tread, treasure, wealth, weapon, weather,
            zealot**

Webster's New Collegiate Dictionary (8th ed.) prefers the pronunciation
bow-kay' but recognizes that *boo-kay'* is also quite common.

short i: **spinach, been, breeches, lettuce, minute**
The -*age* ending: **manage, village (etc.)**
-*feit:* **counterfeit, surfeit, forfeit**
-*eign:* **foreign, sovereign**
-*ui-:* **biscuit, circuit, mannequin, build, guild, guinea**

short o: See *ah,* next chapter.

short u: **blood, flood**
country, couple, cousin, double, enough, rough, slough, touch, tough, trouble, young

During the Middle Ages, the short *o* sound shifted to short *u* in some words, especially before or after the sound *m* or *n*. The spelling *o* survived the change in pronunciation in the following words:

onion, other, oven, accompany, affront, among, brother, color, come, comfort, cover, covert, done, does, dozen, front, govern, honey, hover, love, money, monkey, month, mother, nothing, pommel, shovel, slovenly, smother, somersault, some, son, sponge, stomach, ton, tongue, won, wonder

EXERCISE 45

Cross off the words in the above list in which spelling *ea* for the short *e* sound comes from a word in which the *ea* has the sound long *e*.

EXERCISE 46

List all the homonym pairs represented by a word listed above among the short-vowel sound irregularities.

EXERCISE 47

Correct the misspelled words.

annually	prayrie	wierdness	curfew
arial	coppying	siege	hoax
alley	lieing	magickly	forein
recieve	hygene	tipifying	
payed	tradgical	fruitted	

Chapter Summary

The invasion of words from other languages has created most of the homonyms in English speech. It has also resulted in many variations in spelling, particularly of the long vowel sounds. However, certain spelling generalizations can be made.

1. The most frequent alternate spelling of the long *a* sound is *ai*.

2. Most words spell the long *e* sound *e* or, at the end of a word, *y*. Of the less than 10 percent of words left, most words use the spelling *ee* or *ea*.

3. Long *i* is spelled *y* at the end of a word or before a suffix begining in *i*. It is also spelled *y* in Greek-derived words. If the alternate LVS spelling *ai, ei, oi,* or *ui* comes at the end of a word, its *i* is changed to *y*.

4. The long *o* sound is spelled *o* about 95 percent of the time. The next most popular spelling is *oa*.

5. The letter *u* stands for two sounds, long *u* (often spelled *oo*) and the diphthong *yu* (most often spelled *u*). The pronunciation of long *u* words varies regionally.

Words to Learn

List the heavy-type words you can't spell, as well as the words misspelled in the exercises.

20

Vowel Sounds
from Other Languages

In investigating the makeup of diphthongs, we have introduced the sound *ah,* which is slightly different from the short *o* sound (*cot* vs. *father*) and which didn't often appear alone in early English except as part of the diphthong *i* (ahtee). This *ah* sound and some other vowel sounds came into our language mostly in Invasion words.

Some of those nonnative vowel sounds are made by finding a midway spot between two of our native vowel sounds. Speak the example words aloud until you can figure out how each sound is made.

Common spelling	*Approximate makeup*	*Examples*
a, a(l)	SVS *o* with mouth wide	**car, balm**
o, au, aw, ou	between SVS *o* and SVS *u*	**store, faucet, paw, ought**
oi, oy	above-listed *o* sound + SVS *i*	**foist, coy**
oo	SVS *u* with lips almost closed	**foot, cook**
ou, ow	SVS *a* + SVS *oo* sound above	**ground, how**

The first transcribers of our language couldn't make up their minds how to spell these sounds that had no English equivalent. But some generalizations can be made.

Ah sound as in *car, balm*

The *ah* sound is slightly longer and deeper in the throat than the regular short *o* sound.

144

barb—bob	**heart—hot**	**father—foster**
calm—cob	**mark—mock**	**lava—loft**

The British have a great deal more trouble spelling the sound than we do, because in most regions of the United States we have converted many *ah* words to SVS *a: ask, dance,* etc. In only two general instances (aside from some isolated exceptions) do most of us still retain *ah:* before *r* and before *m* (where a silent *l* is inserted to remind us to use *ah* instead of *a* in pronouncing the word). A list of all the common *a(l)* words appears in Chapter 14, but we'll repeat it here to refresh your memory:

alms	**almond**	**balm**	**calm**
palm	**psalm**	**qualm**	

(Notice that several of these words would have homonyms if we didn't retain the *ah* sound: *bam, cam, Pam.*

Most words that contain the *ah* sound are spelled with *a,* and cause no problems.

arcade	**particular**	**skylark**	**argument**
father	**guard**	**lava**	**camouflage**

(Notice that *guard* doesn't have a *ua* spelling, but a silent *u* that signifies a hard *g* sound.)

It's the very few alternately spelled words that confuse poor spellers, so memorize the following eight exceptions *and spell all the other* ah-*sounding words with* a.

The only three common words spelled *ea:*

heart   hearken   hearth
(and words derived from them)

The only two common words spelled *au:*

aunt   laugh*

The only three common words spelled *ah:*

ah   bah   dahlia*

Aw sound as in *store, faucet*

There are at least four common ways of spelling this sound
—and several other uncommon ways—demonstrating the
trouble the first transcribers had in identifying the sound and
selecting a suitable spelling. Luckily, a few rational patterns
emerge from the mélange.

1. The *aw* sound is most often written simply *a* after the
consonant sound *w* or *kw: (qu):*

quart   warp   reward   water   wharf

2. The *aw* sound is usually written *o* before *r:*

ordinary   mortal   corporal   inform   enormous

Exceptions: the presence of *w* before the sound governs its
spelling more than does an *r* after it (see the examples for
pattern 1).
Also note the following homonyms:

sore—soar	**bore—boar**	**wore—war**
pore—pour	**born—borne**	**worn—warn**
or—ore—oar	**for—fore—four**	**horse—hoarse**

---

*The preferred pronunciation for these words has recently shifted to a
short-a sound (*ant, laff, dal' -ya*), but many people still prefer *ah.*

3. Most other words spell the sound *au,* for example:

author   **taut**   **auction**   **launch**

4. Some words add a helping *e* for no obvious reason:

false	**horse**	**endorse**	**forge**
awe	**corpse**	**remorse**	**gorge**
	before	**indorse**	**corselet**
cause	**gauze**	**applause**	**because**
clause	**pause**	**sauce**	

5. Many one-syllable (and a few two-syllable) words that neither have a *w* before the *aw* sound nor an *r* after it, are spelled *aw.* These words have a distinctive open sound that makes them easy to learn to spell. Have someone test you to eliminate the words you already know how to spell, and memorize the rest.

awe	**awful**	**awning**		
bawl	**bawdy**	**brawl**	**brawn**	
claw	**crawl**	**crawfish**		
dawn	**draw**	**dawdle**	**drawl**	**drawn**
fawn	**flaw**			
gnaw	**gawky**	**guffaw**		
haw	**hawk**	**hawser**	**hawthorn**	
jaw	**law**	**lawn**	**maw**	
paw	**pawn**	**prawn**	**raw**	
saw	**scrawl**	**shawl**	**spawn**	**sprawl**
squaw	**squawk**	**straw**		
thaw	**tawny**	**tawdry**		
yawn	**coleslaw**			

6. Only a few words escape the previous patterns. Memorize these words.

ou: **ought, bought, brought, fought, nought, sought,
       thought, wrought**
oa: **broad, abroad, coarse**
augh: **aught,* caught, daughter, distraught, fraught,
         haughty, naught, naughty, onslaught,
         slaughter, taught**
o: **off, officer**

Oi sound as in *foil*

The sound *oi,* while having no previous equivalent in English, did have a distinctive enough sound that all transcribers were able to agree on a spelling: *oi* if in the middle of a word, and *oy* if at the end. The first rule of making bigger words from small ones applies: if an ending— even a Latin ending—is added, the *y* does not change to *i* since it's part of the vowel cluster *oy*:

employment   joyous   annoyance

In addition, another pattern emerges. See if you can find it by studying the following small chart.

end of word	*preceding vowel*	*preceding consonant*
joy	**loyal**	**toil**
annoy	**royal**	**foist**

Pattern: If the *oi* sound ends a word or precedes a vowel, it is spelled ____. In all other cases, it is spelled ____.

A few words with the *oi* sound contain a helping *e.* The helper is there to help us pronounce the *s* or *c* correctly, not to help the *oi* sound:

choice   voice   rejoice   invoice
poise   noise   turquoise

---

*This word, seldom used any more, means zero, nothing, anything, or all, depending on context.

Short *oo* sound as in *foot*

Though this is a sound distinctive from the *oo* in *food,* it's often spelled the same way. Happily, the sound occurs in only a tiny part of the language and is spelled *oo* or *u* in the vast majority of cases—so learn the few words that don't conform to one of these two choices of spelling and then, if you don't know the spelling, try both *oo* and *u* and let your eye tell you which spelling looks more correct.

Near-homonyms with short *oo* sound

Notice how the *aw* sound in the first word of each pair changes to a short *oo* sound in the second word:

yore—your   **tore—tour**   **shore—sure**   **door—dour**

(Notice that, before the consonant *r,* the vowel sound is slightly changed.)

Some common irregularly spelled short *oo* sound words

    eu: **pleurisy***
    o: **bosom, wolf, woman**
    oui: **bouillon**
    ou: **amour, camouflage, could, contour, courier,**
           detour, gourmet, paramour, should,
           tambourine, tour, tournament, troubadour,
           would, your*
    uo: **fluorescent***

Ow sound as in *how*

There are only two spellings for the *ow* sound: *ow* and *ou.*

---

*A number of these Invasion words are slowly changing in pronunciation to the *aw* or *schwa* sound, especially when the short *oo* is followed by *r.*

Ow is most often used at the end of a word:

cow   endow   chow

However, it also appears in many other common words, especially when followed closely by an *l* sound, an *n* sound, or an *r* sound:

avowal	clown	shower	dowager
jowl	down	bower	chowder
fowl	gown	flower	powder
howl	renown	tower	rowdy
cowl	town	lower*	dowdy
towel	brown	power	prowess
bowel	crown	glower	howitzer
dowel	drown	bowery	drowsy
prowl	frown		browse
growl		coward	dowry
scowl	vowel	trowel	

If the word doesn't end in an *ow* sound, and isn't on the above list, you're probably correct if you spell the sound *ou*.

A final word

It's done! It's over! You've learned to spell 99 percent of all the words you'll ever need. If you've gone slowly, absorbed all the patterns, and memorized the exceptions, you're now among the ranks of the very best spellers.

Stash the book in a safe place, so that if you ever need a refresher course you can pull it out again. We've put you on the road to good spelling. The rest is up to you.

We wish you a happy journey and a safe harbor at the end.

---

*Don't confuse this word, pronounced *low'-er* to rhyme with *power* and meaning "to frown or look gloomy," with the more common word pronounced *loh'-er.*

Chapter Summary

1. The sound *ah* which appears most often before the letter *r,* is usually spelled *a.* Before the letter *m* it is spelled *a* + silent *l.*
2. The sound *aw* is most often spelled:
   a after the consonant sound *w* or *kw* (*qu*),
   o before the sound *r,*
   aw at the end of a word (and within a few words), and
   au in most other cases.
3. If the sound *oi* ends a word or precedes a vowel, it is spelled *oy.* In all other cases, it is spelled *oi.*
4. The short *oo* sound, as in *foot,* is spelled *oo* in most cases.
5. The sound *ow* as in *how* is spelled *ow* most often at the end of a word and before the sounds *l, n,* and *r.* In most other cases, it is spelled *ou.*

Words to Learn

List this chapter's demons and misspelled words for study.

BIBLIOGRAPHY

Alfred, Ruel A. *Spelling: The Application of Research Findings*. Washington, DC: National Education Association, 1977.

Balmuth, Miriam. *The Roots of Phonics, a Historical Introduction*. New York: McGraw-Hill, 1982.

Brain, Joseph J. *The Blue Book of Spelling and Dictionary Study*. New York: Regents, 1960.

Chomsky, Noam, and Morris Halle. *The Sound Pattern of English*. New York: Harper & Row, 1968.

Dewey, Godfred. *English Spelling: Roadblock to Reading*. New York: Teachers College Press, 1971.

Dewey, Godfred. *Relative Frequency of English Spellings*. New York: Teachers College Press, 1970.

Dolch, Edward W. *The Modern Teaching of Spelling*. Champaign, IL: Garrard, 1950.

Gibson, Byron H. *Word Power: A Short Guide to Vocabulary and Spelling*. Deland, FL: Everett/Edwards, 1966.

Hall, Jr., Robert A. *Sound and Spelling in English*. Philadelphia: Chilton, 1961.

Hanna, Paul R.; Hodges, Richard E.; and Hanna, Jean S. *Spelling: Structure and Strategies*. Boston: Houghton Mifflin, 1971.

Hanna, Paul R.; Hodges, Richard E.; Hanna, Jean S.; and Rudorf, Erwin H. Jr., *Phoneme-Grapheme Correspondences as Cues to Spelling Improvement*, OE-32008. Washington, DC: U.S. Department of Health, Education, and Welfare, 1966.

Personke, Carl; and Yee, Albert H. *Comprehensive Spelling Instruction: Theory, Research, and Application.* Scranton, PA: Intext, 1971.

Smelt, Elsie D. *Speak, Spell and Read English, 2nd edition.* Victoria, Australia: Longman, Hawthorn, 1976.

Thomas, Charles Kenneth. *An Introduction to the Phonetics of American English.* New York: Ronald Press, 1947.

Williams, Ralph M. *Phonetic Spelling for College Students.* New York: Oxford University Press, 1960.

APPENDIX A

A Directory of Spelling Demons
Words that are homonyms are starred (*)

Included here are most of the words in the book that we specifically called to your attention. Add your *own* misspelled words from your end-of-chapter lists, and from other writing sources, to make this directory truly your own.

abreast	accumulate	adieu	agenda
abridgment	accurate	adjacent	aggravate
abroad	accusation	adjective	aggregate
abscess	accustom	adjourn	aggression
absentee	ache	adjunct	agile
abyss	achieve	adjust	agitate
acacia	acknowledgment	adolescent	agree
academician	acoustic	advantageous	agreeable
accede	acquaint	advertise	ah
accelerator	acquiesce	advise	ahead
accept	acquire	adz	aid*
accessible	acquit	aerial	aide*
accidentally	acreage	aesthetic	ail*
accommodate	acronym	affect	air*
accompany	action	affix	aisle*
accord	active	affront	ajar
account	ad*	afterwards	alchemy
accountant	add*	again	ale*
accrue	addressee	against	algae

alias
alien
align
alkaline
all*
allege
allegiance
allegro
allot
allotment
allotted
allotting
allow
almond
alms
alpha
although
amateur
amazon
amethyst
amoeba
among
amorphous
amour
amphibian
amphitheater
amputee
anachronism
analysis
analytic
analyze
anarchy
anathema
ancestor
anchor
ancient
andante

angry
anguish
anneal
annex
annihilate
annoyance
answer
antagonism
antic
antique
antonym
anxiety
anxious
apex
aplomb
apogee
apostle
apostrophe
apparatus
apparent
apparition
appeal
appear
appease
appendix
applause
apple
appointment
appreciable
appreciate
approach
approve
apt
aquarium
aquatic
archaic
archetype

architect
archive
arctic
arduous
armor
armoring
arousal
arraign
arrangement
artesian
artificial
artiste
as
ascend
ascetic
Asia
askance
asphalt
assassin
assiduous
assign
associate
association
assume
asylum
ate*
atrocious
atrophy
attractive
auctioneer
audacious
aught*
augur
aunt
auspicious
autonomy
autumn

avaricious
avid
avowal
aware
awe*
awful
awl*
awning
awry
ax
axiom
axis
axle
azalea
bachelor
bah
bait*
balk
ballet
ballot
balloting
balm
banquet
bare*
baring
barrel
barreling
barring
basin
bate*
batiste
battalion
bawdy
bawl
bayou
bazooka
beacon

beagle
beaker
bear*
beat*
beau*
beautician
beauty
beaver
because
becoming
bedraggled
been*
beet*
beetle
before
begin
beginning
behalf
beige
believe
beneath
beneficial
benefit
benefiting
benign
bent
bequeath
bereave
beseech
besiege
between
bicycle
bin*
bite*
blank
blaspheme
blasphemy

blatant
blew*
blight
blizzard
bloat
blood
bludgeon
blue*
boar*
board*
boast
boat
bogus
bolero
bomb
bookkeeper
bore*
bored*
born*
borne*
borough
bosom
bought
bouillon
boulder
boulevard
bouquet
bow*
bowel
bower
bowery
box
braise
brake*
brassiere
brawl
brawn

bread*
breadth*
break*
breast
breath*
bred*
breeches
breeze
brew
bridal*
bridle*
brief
brigadier
bright
bristle
broach
broad
broccoli
brochure
bronchial
bronchitis
brooch
brother
brought
brown
browse
bruise
buccaneer
build
built
bulkhead
bulldoze
bulletin
bungalow
buoy
bureau
burnt

bury
bustle
business
busyness
but*
butt*
buxom
buy*
buys
buzz
buzzard
by*
bye*
byte*
cafe
calf
calk
calm
calypso
camouflage
campaign
camphor
candidate
candidly
candor
cannot
canoe
cantaloupe
canteen
canvas*
canvass*
capacious
capital*
capitol*
caprice
capricious
carburetor

careen	chaise	choirmaster	clinician
careworn	chalk	choo*	clip
caribou	chamberpot	chord*	clique
carouse	chameleon	chorus	cloak
carousel	champagne	chowder	clothing
carousing	chandelier	christen	clown
carrying	changeable	Christmas	clue
cartridge	changing	chromatic	coach
casino	chaos	chrome	coal
castle	character	chronic	coalesce
cataclysm	chargeable	chronicle	coarse*
catastrophe	chassis	chronology	coast
caught	chasm	chronometer	coat
causal	chasten	chrysalis	coax
cause	chastise	chump	cobbler
cavalier	chattel	chute*	cocoa
cayenne	chauffeur	cigar	coercion
cede*	cheap*	cipher	coleslaw
ceiling	cheep*	circuit	colleague
celebrity	chef	circuitous	collect
cellestial	chemical	circumference	collecting
cello	chemise	circumvent	college
cellophane	chenile	cistern	cologne
cement	chestnut	citation	color
cemetery	chew*	cite*	colossal
censure	chickadee	citizen	column
cent*	chief	citywide	coma
centennial	chiffonier	civic	comb
centrifugal	chimera	civilian	come
centurion	chimneypot	civility	comet
ceramic	chintz	clause*	comfort
cerebral	chiropractor	claws*	comma
cerebrum	chisel	cleanly	commercial
certain	chlorine	cleanse	commiserate
certificate	chloroform	cleavage	commit
cessation	chlorophyll	cleft	competent
chagrin	choir	climb	complement[1]

complex
compliment*
compromise
conceal
concede
conceit
conceive
concerto
conch
concussion
concussive
condemn
confident
congeal
congress
conjecture
connect
connecting
conqueror
conquest
conscience
conscious
consensus
consider
considering
consign
consistent
console
consoling
construction
construe
contemptible
context
contour
convalescence
convey
coo*

cookbook
coordinate
cord*
cordial
corner
corporation
corps
corpse
corral
corralled
corralling
corrals
correspond
corrupt
corrupting
corselet
costly
coterie
cougar
could
coulee
council*
councillor*
counsel*
counselor*
counterfeit
country
coup*
couple
coupon
courageous
courier
course*
cousin
cover
covet
coward

cowl
coyote
cozy
crawfish
crawl
creak*
creature
credible
credulous
creek*
crepe
crept
crescendo
crescent
criticism
critique
crochet
croquet
croup
crowd
crown
crucial
crucifixion
cruise
crumb
crustacean
crutches
crypt
crystal
cudgel
cue
curbing
curfew
curvaceous
cyanide
cybernetics
cycle

cyclone
cyclonic
cylinder
cylindrical
cymbal*
cynic
cynosure
cypress
cyst
czar
dahlia
dam*
damn*
daughter
dazzle
deacon
dead
deaf
dealt
dearly
death
debt
deceased
deceit
deceive
decided
deciduous
decision
decrease
decree
defeat
defer
deference
deferred
deferring
definite
degree

deign
delicious
delight
demean
demeanor
demur
demurrage
demurred
denunciate
dependent
deposit
deposition
depreciate
descend
descendant
describe
description
desert
design
desirable
despair
desperate
dessert
detour
deuce
device
devil
devise
devising
devotee
dew*
dexterous
diaphragm
dichotomy
die*
difference
different

diffraction
dilapidated
diner
dinner
disappear
disappearing
disaster
disastrous
discern
discernible
disciple
discipline
discreet
discussion
disease
disestablishment
disobey
disparate
displease
disposal
dispossess
dissent
dissimilar
dissimulate
dissolve
distraught
distribute
diva
divers*
diverse*
diversion
divide
divine
division
dizzy
do*
does

dolphin
done*
door
double
doubt
dough
dour
dowry
doze
dozen
dread
dreamt
drew
drivel
drizzle
drown
drowsy
dryad
dual*
duchess
due*
duel*
dumb
dun*
dungaree
dungeon
dye*
dyeing*
dying*
dynamic
dynamite
dynamo
dynasty
dysentery
eagle
easel
easy

ecclesiastical
echelon
echo
ecstasy
eczema
educate
eerie
effect
effervesce
efficacious
efficient
egg
eight*
either
electrician
electrolyte
elephant
eligible
eliminate
elite
elixir
emaciate
embalm
embalming
embarrass
embezzle
emphasis
emphatic
employment
encouragement
encroach
encyclopedia
endeavor
endorse
engineer
enough
enrich

ensign
enterprise
entreat
entree
enunciate
envisage
enzyme
ephemeral
epistle
epoch
equal
equivalent
ere*
err*
especially
essay
essential
esteem
eulogy
eunuch
euphemism
euphoria
evil
eviscerate
ewe*
exaggerate
exceed
excel
excellent
except
excerpt
excess
excise
excite
excruciate
exercise
exhaust

exhibit
exhilarate
exhilaration
exhort
exist
existing
exorcise
explicit
exquisite
extension
extensive
eye*
facial
faint*
fair*
fairy
fallacious
false
fare*
fascinate
fascism
fasten
fate*
fathom
fatigue
fawn
faze*
feasible
feat*
feather
feature
feeble
feet*
feign
feint*
feisty
felt

ferocious
ferry
fervent
fete*
feud
few
fez
fiasco
fictitious
fiddle
fidget
fiduciary
fie
fief
field
fiend
fierce
fifth
fight
figurine
filigree
final
finale
finally
financial
financier
fix
fixedness
fizz
fizzle
flaw
flecks*
fledgling
flew*
flex*
flexible
flit

float
flood
floor
fluorescent
flower
flue*
flux
foal
foam
focus
folk
follower
fondness
fondue
food
for*
fore*
forehead
foreign
forfeit
forge
forget
forgetting
formally
formerly
forte
forth*
fought
fourth*
fowl
fox
framework
franchise
frantically
franticly (alt. sp.)
fraudulent
fraught

frazzle	gesture	graham	gypsy
freeze*	get	grandee	gyrate
freight	geyser	grandeur	gyroscope
frenzy	ghetto	grandmother	hail*
frequent	ghost	grapefruit	hale*
fricassee	ghostly	graph	half
friend	ghoul	gray (also: grey)	halve
frieze*	gingerbread	grate*	handkerchie
fright	gist	great*	harpsichord
frizz	gizzard	greediness	hasten
frizzled	glacial	grenadier	haughty
fro	glaciate	grew	hauteur
frond	glandular	grey (also: gray)	hawk
front	glisten	grieve	hawser
frontier	gloat	grievous	hawthorn
frown	glower	grind	hazel
froze	glue	gristle	head
fruit	glycerin	grizzled	headache
fungi	gnarled	groan*	heal*
furlough	gnash	grog	health
fusion	gnat	group	hearken
fuzz	gnaw	grovel	heart
gadget	gnome	growl	heartache
gage*	gnu*	grown*	hearth
gait*	goad	growth	heathen
galaxy	goal	grudging	heather
gale	goat	gruesome	heaven
gallop	gopher	guarantee	heavy
galloping	gorge	guffaw	heel*
gate*	gorgeous	guild	heifer
gauche	goulash	guileless	height
gauge*	gourmet	guinea	heinous
gauze	govern	guy	heir*
gawky	gown	guzzle	herb
generally	gracious	gym	herbaceous
genteel	gradual	gyp	hew
geography	graduate	gypsum	hex

hexagon	hydrochloric	index	jazz
hi*	hydrogen	indict	jealous
hie*	hydrolics	indigestible	jeep
high*	hygiene	individual	jeer
him*	hymn*	inertia	jejune
his	hyperbola	inexorable	jelly
hoar*	hypercritical	infer	jeopardy
hoarse*	hyphen	inference	jest
hoary	hypnotize	inferred	jet
hoax	hypocrisy	influx	jettison
hold*	hypocrite	inhumane	jewel
hole*	hypothesis	initiation	jib
holed*	idiosyncrasy	innate	jiffy
holistic	idyllic	innocent	jiggle
hollowness	I'll*	innocuous	jilt
honest	imagine	inquire	jimmy
honey	imbue	inquiring	jingle
honeyed	impale	inquisition	jive
honor	impassable	insert	jostle
hoop*	impeach	inserting	jowl
horizon	imperative	insouciance	joyous
horse*	imposition	instead	jubilee
hours*	impression	instinct	judgment
hover	impressive	insurance	judicial
howitzer	improvisation	intelligent	judicious
howl	improvise	intensive	juice
hubbub	impugne	intention	juxtapose
hubcap	inane	intoxicate	kale
huddling	inchoate	intrigue	kaleidoscope
hue*	incision	inveigle	kangaroo
hump	incompatible	irascible	kaput
hussar	incongruity	irresistible	kayak
hussy	increase	island	kazoo
hustle	incredible	isle*	kept
hyacinth	incur	jam*	key*
hybrid	indeed	jamb*	keyed
hydrant	independent	jaw	khaki

kilo	leafless	lobber	maneuver
kindest	leak*	lobster	mannequin
knack	lean*	lode*	mantel*
knapsack	leapt	logician	mantle*
knave	leather	lone*	maraschino
knead*	leaven	loquacious	margarine
knee	led*	lose	marquee
kneel	leek*	louver	marriage
knell	left	love	masochist
knelt	legible	lovely	masthead
knew*	legion	lower	mathematician
knife	leisure	loyal	matinee
knight*	leopard	luscious	matrix
knit*	leprechaun	luxury	mauve
knob	lettuce	lyceum	maw
knock	levee	lye*	maxim
knoll	lewd	lymph	maximum
knot*	liable*	lynch	mayonnaise
know*	liaison	lynx	maze*
knowledge	libel*	lyre	mazurka
knuckle	lichen	lyric	meadow
knurl	lie*	machine	meager
lain*	liege	made*	mean*
lamb	lien*	magazine	meant
lament	lieu	magician	measles
lamenting	lieutenant	magpie	measure
lane*	light	maid*	meat*
larynx	limb	mail*	mechanic
later	limousine	main*	medal*
latex	liquid	maize*	meddle*
latter	lira	male*	meet*
laugh	listen	malfeasance	melancholy
law	load*	malice	melee
lawn	loaf	malicious	membrane
lax	loam	malign	memorandum
laxative	loan*	manage	mendacious
lead*	loath	mane*	merchandise

meretricious	month	neither	nuzzle
merger	morphology	neophyte	nymph
mesa	mortgage	nephew	oak
metal	mortician	nephritis	oar*
metamorphose	mosaic	nestle	oat
metaphor	mosquito	neurotic	oath
mew	mote*	neuter	obey
mien*	mother	neutral	objective
might*	motif	neutron	oblique
mildew	motion	nevertheless	obscene
militant	mould*	new*	obscure
minute	move	news	obsolescent
miscellaneous	movie	newt	obstetrician
miscible	much	next	occasion
misinform	murmur	niece	occasionally
misspell	muscle*	night*	occupation
mistletoe	musician	nine	occur
misty	mussel*	nineteen	occurred
mite*	mustache	ninety	occurrence
mitt	muzzle	ninth	occurring
mix	myriad	nisei	ocean
mnemonic	mystery	nit	ocher
moan	mystic	nitrogenous	octave
moat*	myth	no*	odd
mobile	naive	nominee	off
moccasin	nasal	nonchalant	officer
model	nascent	nonnative	official
modulate	naught	not*	officious
modulus	(also: nought)	nothing	often
moisten	naughty	nougat	oh*
mold*	nausea	nought	ohm
monarch	nay*	(also: naught)	okay
money	necessary	novel	omission
monied	need*	noxious	omit
monk	needle	nozzle	omniscience
monkey	negligee	nuisance	onion
monkeyshines	neigh*	numb	onslaught

onyx
ooze
opaque
or*
orange
orchestra
orchid
ordeal
ore*
orphan
orthodox
oscillate
oscilloscope
other
ought*
ours*
outrageous
oven
overrun
overwhelm
owe*
ox
oxide
oxygen
pachyderm
pail*
pair*
pal
pale*
pallid
palm
pampas
pamphlet
panic
panicked
panicking
panicky

paprika
parachute
paradox
paralytic
paralyze
paramecium
paramour
paraphernalia
paraphrase
pare*
parliament
parochial
particularly
partisan
partridge
patrician
pause*
paws*
peace*
peacock
peak*
peal*
pear*
peasant
pediatrician
pedigree
peek*
peel*
peevish
pendulum
people
perceive
percentage
perigee
permanent
permissible
pernicious

perplex
perplexity
persistent
perspicacious
pervade
pestle
petal
petite
pew
phaeton
phalanx
phallic
phantasm
phantasmagoria
pharmacy
pharynx
phase*
pheasant
phenomenon
philanthropy
philharmonic
philosophy
phlegm
phlegmatic
phobia
phoebe
phoenix
phone
phosphate
phosphorescent
phosphorus
photo
phrase
phrenetic
phylum
physical
physician

physics
pi*
piazza
piccolo
picnic
picnicked
picnicker
picnicking
pie*
piece*
piecemeal
pierce
piquant
pique*
pistachio
pistol
plaid
plain*
plane*
planed
planned
plateau
pleasant
plebiscite
pleurisy
plight
plum*
plumb*
plump
pluralism
pneumatic
pneumonia
poach
police
politician
polka
poltergeist

polygamy	prestigious	pseudo	quiz
pommel	pretext	pseudonym	quizzes
pore*	prevail	pseudopod	quizzical
porridge	prevailing	psoriasis	raccoon
possess	prevalent	psyche	racial
possession	prey*	psychiatry	rack*
possessive	pries*	psychic	racketeer
possessor	priest	psycho	rain*
posthumous	principal*	psychoanalysis	raise*
poultice	principle*	psychology	rancor
poultry	privilege	psychosomatic	rap*
pour*	prize*	pterodactyl	rapacious
powder	procedural	ptomaine	rascal
power	procedure	publicly	raspberry
praise	proceed	pupil	raw
pram	procession	purr	raze*
prawn	processive	pursue	razor
pray*	profess	pursuit	read*
precede	proffer	purvey	ready
precedence	proffering	puzzle	real*
precedent	profit*	pygmy	realm
precious	profiteer	pylon	reason
precocious	prominent	pyramid	rebel
predict	propel	pyre	rebelling
predicting	propellant	pyrite	recede
preexist	prophet*	pyromania	receipt
prefer	prophylactic	pyrotechnics	receive
preference	prosaic	python	reciprocity
preferential	proscenium	qualm	recommend
preferred	proselyte	quark	reconsidered
preferring	prototype	quartz	red*
prefix	prove	quay*	reddish
prejudicial	provincial	queasy	redeem
prepossessing	prowess	questionnaire	reed*
prescience	prowl	quiescent	reedit
presidents	proximity	quiet	reek*
prestige	psalm	quite	reel*

reenact	rescue	roar	scale
referee	residual	roast	scenario
reflex	resign	rode*	scene*
reflexive	rest*	rosary	scent*
refugee	restaurant	rosin	scepter
refute	resuscitate	rote*	schedule
refuting	retch*	rouge	scheme
regale	retire	rough	schism
regime	retiring	roulette	schizophrenia
reign*	retreat	route	scholar
rein*	reveal	routine	school
reindeer	revenue	rowdy	schooner
reject	reverie	royal	science
relate	revise	rue	scintillate
relax	rhapsody	rung*	scion
release	rheostat	rupee	scissors
relieve	rhetoric	rustle	scowl
religious	rheumatic	rye*	scrawl
relinquish	rheumatism	sacrificial	screw
reload	rhinestone	saffron	scythe
remark	rhinoceros	sagacious	sea*
remarkable	rhododendron	said	seam*
remarking	rhomboid	sail*	seas*
remorse	rhubarb	salacious	see*
renaissance	rhyme*	sale*	seed*
renew	rhythm	salient	seem*
renown	rich	saline	seen*
repartee	ricochet	salmon	sees*
repeal	rift	salve	seismic
repeat	right*	sapling	seize*
repellent	rime*	sarcasm	sensitive
replies	ring*	satchel	sensual
reprieve	rite*	satellite	sent*
reproach	roach	sauce	sepulcher
required	road*	saw	seraphim
requisite	roam	saxophone	settee
rescind	roan	says	seventh

sew*	ski	soulful	stein
sewer	skulk	soup	stew
sex	skull	souvenir	stile*
sextant	skunk	sovereign	stomach
shaft	slaughter	spacious	stonecutter
shale	slay*	spawn	straight*
sharecropper	sleigh*	spearmint	strait*
shawl	sleight*	special	strap
sheik	slept	species	stratagem
shepherd	sleuth	specious	strategy
shield	slew	speculative	straw
shoal	slight*	spent	streamer
shoe	slop	sphinx	strew
shone*	slough (also: sluff)	spinach	stripling
shoot*	slovenly	sponge	strumming
shore	sluice	spongy	strumpet
should	smooth	sprawl	strut
shovel	smother	spread	style*
shower	sneeze	squaw	stylus
shown*	so*	squawk	subject
shrewd	soap	squeamish	submarginally
shriek	soar*	squeegee	subpoena
shrivel	social	squeeze	subtle
siege	sodajerk	staccato	succeed
sigh	soften	stair*	succor
sighs*	solder	stalk	succumb
sight*	sole*	standardize	such
sign	solemn	stake*	suede
similar	soloing	stare*	suffrage
sinew	some*	statistician	sugar
site*	somersault	stead	suit
six	son*	steak*	sum*
size*	soothe	steal*	summons
sizzle	sophisticated	stealth	sun*
skate	sore*	steel*	sunk
skein	sought	steeple	superficial
skewer	soul*	steersman	superintendent

supersede
supervise
sure
surely
surfeit
surreptitious
survey
susceptible
suspicion
suspicious
swastika
swear
sweat
swept
swivel
sword
sycamore
syllable
syllogism
sylvan
symbiosis
symbol*
symmetry
sympathy
symphony
symptom
synagogue
synchronize
syphilis
syringe
syrup
system
tableau
tacks*
tail*
talc
talcum

tale*
tambourine
target
targeting
tassel
taught*
taut*
tawdry
tawny
tax*
taxi
taxidermy
team*
tear
technical
technician
technique
teem*
teeter
televise
tenacious
tenseness
tension
tepee
text
textile
texture
thank
thaw
their*
theirs*
therapeutic
there*
there's*
they
they're*
thief

thigh
thistle
thorough
though
thought
thousand
thousandths
thread
threat
threw*
throat
through*
thumb
thyme*
tie
time*
timpani
tincture
to*
toad
toast
tobacco
toccata
tomb
ton
tongue
too*
toothache
topaz
tore*
torque
touch
tough
tour*
tournament
towards
towel

tower
town
toxic
toxin
tranquil
transcend
transfer
transferring
transit
trapeze
treachery
tread
treason
treasure
treatise
treatment
treaty
trestle
tries
trim
trimly
trimmed
trio
triumph
triumvirate
troop*
trophy
troubadour
trouble
troupe*
trousseau
trowel
true
trussed*
trust*
trustee
trusty

tryst	usage	wail*	wheat
tubeless	vacuum	waist*	wheedle
tunnel	vain*	wait*	wheel
tunneling	vale*	waive*	wheeze
turquoise	vane*	walk	when
twitched	vanquish	waltz	where*
two*	vary	wanly	whet*
tycoon	vehement	war*	whether*
type	vehicle	ware*	whew*
typhoid	veil*	warn*	whey*
typhoon	vein*	was	which*
typhus	veneer	wasp	whiff
typical	vengeance	waste*	while*
typically	verdure	watt*	whim
typify	very	wave*	whimper
typographic	vessel	wax*	whimsy
tyranny	vestige	way*	whine*
tyrant	vex	weak*	whinny
tyro	vice*	wealth	whip
ukulele	viceroy	weapon	whirl*
uncap	vicious	wear*	whisk
uncle	vie	weary	whiskey
unconfidential	view	weasel	whisper
unconventional	village	weather*	whistle
uncouth	viola	week*	whit*
undulate	viscount	weevil	white
ungracious	vise*	weigh*	whither
unhelpful	visit	weight*	whittle
unique	vivacious	weird	whiz
universally	vixen	wept	who
unnecessary	vizier	western	whole*
unpeel	vodka	wet*	wholly*
unpeeling	volunteer	whacks*	whom
unseemly	voracious	whale*	whoop*
unusually	vortex	whalebone	whore*
upheaval	vowel	wharf	whorl*
urgent	voyage	what*	whose

why	wore*	wrist	yoke*
width	worn*	write*	yolk*
wield	worth	writhe	yore*
wile*	would*	written	you*
wine*	wound	wrong	young
wing	wrack*	wrote*	your*
wink	wrangle	wrought	youth
wished	wrap*	wrung*	yucca
wit*	wrath	wry*	zealot
witch*	wreak*	yacht	zebra
withheld	wreath	yankee	zero
wolf	wreck	yawn	zest
woman	wren	yelp	zinc
womb	wrench	yen	zip
women	wrest*	yew*	zipper
won*	wrestle	yield	zone
wonder	wretch*	yippee	zoo
wood*	wriggle	yodel	
wordfinder	wring*	yogi	

APPENDIX B

Greek- and Latin-Derived, Prefixes, Suffixes, and Roots

LATIN-DERIVED PREFIXES

Prefix	Meaning
ab-	from, away, off
ad-	to, toward, for
ambi-	around, about
ante-	before
bene-	well
circum-	around, about
con-, com-, co-	with, together, together with (also used to mean *very*)
contra-, counter-	against, in opposition
de-	down, off, away, from
dis-, di-	apart, not, in different directions
ex-, e-	out, out of, from, off, forth, without (also used to mean *very*)
extra-	outside, outside of

Prefix	Meaning
in-, en-, ir-	in, on, upon, into, toward, against, out (also used to mean *not*)
inter-	between
intra-, intro-	within
mis-	badly, bad
ne-	not
ob-, obs-, oc-, op-, of-	to, toward, for, against, meeting, in the way, hindering, veiling (also used to mean *very*)
pen-, pene-	almost
per-, pel-, par-, pil-	through, by (also used to mean *very*)
post-	after
prae-, pre-	before, previous, ahead, in advance, surpassing
pro-, por-, pur-	in front of, forth, for, instead of
re-, red-	back to, backward, again (also used to mean *very*)
retro-	back, backward, behind
se-	apart, without, aside
sub-, suc-, sug-, suf-, sup-, sus-	under, below, from below, lower, in secret, in addition, instead
super-, sover-, sur-	above, over
trans-, tra-, tres-, tre-	across, over, beyond, through, into a different state or place
ultra-	beyond
un-	not

LATIN-DERIVED SUFFIXES

Suffix	Used for
-a	noun ending (*coma, drama*)
-able, -ible	adjective ending (*passable, impossible*)
-ain	noun ending (*mountain, villain*)
-al	adjective ending (*dual, equal*)
-al, -el, -le, -ol	noun ending (*medal, fuel, article, symbol*)
-an	noun ending (*human, sultan*)
-ance, -ence	noun ending (*maintenance, influence*)
-ant, -ent	adjective ending (*jubilant, dissident*)
-ar	adjective ending (*similar, circular*)
-ary	adjective ending (*primary, culinary*)
-ate	verb ending with long *a* sound (*educate, confiscate*)
-ate	adjective ending with short *a* sound (*accurate, private*)
-en	verb, adjective, or noun ending (*happen, swollen, omen*)
-er, -or, -ar	noun ending: one who, one that (*printer, actor, molar*)
ern	verb, noun, or adjective ending (*govern, lantern, eastern*)
-ery, -ory	noun ending (*nunnery, category*)
-et	noun ending (*garret, facet*)
-ic	noun ending (*tonic, clinic*)
-ice	noun ending (*cowardice, malice*)

Suffix	Used for
-id	adjective ending (*valid, horrid*)
-ify	verb ending (*vivify, codify*)
-il, -ile	noun, adjective ending (*peril, facile*)
-in	noun ending (*origin, chagrin*)
-ine	verb, adjective, or noun ending (*determine, bovine, fluorine*)
-ior	adjective or noun ending (*anterior, senior*)
-ious, -eous	adjective ending (*audacious, spontaneous*)
-ise, -ize	verb ending (*chastise, analyze*)
-is	noun ending (*synthesis, thesis*)
-ish	verb ending (*cherish, perish*)*
-it, -ite	noun ending (*credit, finite*)
-ity	noun ending (*infinity, charity*)
-ive	noun, adjective ending (*missive, active*)
-on	noun ending (*eon, talon*)
-or	noun ending (*favor, odor*)
-ous	adjective ending (*callous, zealous*)
-ot	noun ending (*chariot, argot*)
-tory	noun ending (*laboratory, territory*)
-ure	verb or noun ending (*injure, measure*)
-us	noun ending (*focus, chorus*)

---

*Note that the Latin *-ish* ending is a verb ending, while the native English *ish* is an adjective ending (*churlish, devilish*).

GREEK-DERIVED PREFIXES

Prefix	Meaning
a-, an-	not, without
amphi-, amph-	both, of both sides, on both sides, around
ana-, an-	up, upward, backward, again, anew (also used to mean *very*)
anti-, ant-, anth-	opposite, against, rivaling, in exchange
apo-, ap-, aph-	from, away from, off, quite
arch-	chief, leading
auto-	self
di-, dy-	two, twice
dia-, di-	through, between, apart, across
dys-	ill, bad, difficult
ek-, ex-	out, out of
el-, em-, en-	in, into
epi-, ep-, eph-	upon, at, for (of time), to, on the ground of, in addition to
eu-, ev-	well, good, advantageous
gymn-, gymno-	naked, bare
homeo-	similar
homo-	same
hyper-	over, above, beyond, exceedingly, excessive
hypo-, hyp-, hyph-	under, below, slightly
isos-	equal

Prefix	Meaning
kata-, kat-, kath-	down, away, concerning (also used to mean *very*)
meta-, met-, meth-	with, after, beyond, over, change
ortho-	straight, right, true
paleo-	old
para-, par-	beside, beyond, contrary to, amiss, irregular
peri-	around, about, near
pro-	before, in front of
pros-	to, toward, in addition
syn-, sym-, syl-, sys-	with, along with, together, like
tri-	three times

GREEK-DERIVED SUFFIXES

Suffix	Meaning
-archy	rule by
-cracy	rule by
-ectomy	cutting out of
-eum, -aeum	place for
-gram	thing written or drawn
-graph, -graphy	writing
-isk	a little, little

Suffix	Meaning
-ism	state of, attachment to, belief in, practice of
-ist	one concerned with, one who adheres to, one who believes in
-ite	one having to do with, inhabitant of, descendent of (also used to form names of chemicals, minerals, etc.)
-itis	inflammation of
-ity	quality of, state of
-ium, -ion	thing connected with (also used to mean *little*)
-ize	to make into or like, to subject to, to put into conformity with
-logy	collection of, study of, science of
-m, -ma, -me	act of, state of, result of
-mancy	foretelling by
-oid	like, resembling
-oma	morbid affection for
-osis	process of, disease connected with
-se, -sis, -sy	act of, state of
-t, -te, -tes	one who, that which
-ter, -tery, -terion	place for, means for, instrument for
-tomy	cutting, cutting of
-ton	thing that is
-urgy	art of working

LATIN-DERIVED ROOTS

Root	Meaning
acerb	harsh, bitter
acu	needle, sharp
adipi	fat
agri, ager	field
albu	white
alt	high
amen	pleasant, charming
angu	angle, corner
anima	air, breath, life, soul
an	old woman
ann	year
apex, apic	point, top
aqua	water
arma	arms
ars, art	skill, art
artu, art	joint
ater, atri	black
aur	gold
barba	beard
bell	war, pretty
bene	well
bon	good
capit	head

Root	Meaning
carp, carpt, cerpt	pick, pluck
car	dear
cede	go, yield
cel	sky
cept, capt	take, hold, grasp
cert	sure
circ	about, around, ring
commun	common
cor, cord	heart
corp	body
cred, credit	believe
culpa	fault, blame
cura	care, trouble, attention
curv	bent, curved
dens, dent	tooth
edi	building, house
ego	I
equ	equal
estu	heat, tide
exter	outside
facie	appearance, surface, shape, face
fact	make, do
ferru	iron
ferus	wild, untamed

Root	Meaning
fest	joyful
fide	trust, faith
fini	limit, boundary, end
firm	fixed, steadfast
flor	flower
form	shape
fort	strong
fortu	fate, fortune
fum	smoke, steam
funer	death, funeral
fusc	dark
gelid	icy cold
gens, gent, genu, gener	tribe, race, kind, sort
gradu, gress, gredi	step, degree
gratu	pleasing, grateful, agreeable
grav	heavy
homo	man
hosp	host, guest
host	enemy, sacrifice
infer	under
inter, itiner	journey
ipse	self, own
iter	again
jur, jus	law, right

Root	Meaning
juv	young man, young
labor	work
latus, lati	wide
latus, later	side
laud	praise
liber	free, unrestrained
locu	place
luci	light
magn	great
mal	bad
manu	hand
mens, ment	mind
met, metu	fear
misc	mingle
miti	mild, soft
mode	measure, method, fashion
mors, mort	death
mos, mori	habit, custom
mund	earth, the world
munu, mun	duty, gift, reward
ne	not
nef	sin, impious deed
niger, nigr	black
nihil	nothing

Root	Meaning
noct	night
norm	measure, standard, pattern
noster, nostr	our
nov	new
nox	harm
null	none
omni	all
onus, oner	burden
oper	work
ops, opis	influence, wealth
ordo, ordin	order, regular succession
par, pari	equal
pars, part	portion
pauc	few
pen	nearly, almost
pes, pedis	foot
pesti	disease, plague
plan	level, flat
pleb	common people
plus, plur	more
port, portu	harbor, port
post	coming after, following
primu	first
radi	root
re, res	thing, matter

Root	Meaning
rect	upright, straight
regn	government, rule
ruber, rubri	red
sacer, sacri	sacred
sign	mark, token
solu	alone, single
somn	sleep
son	sound
suc	juice, sap, taste
super	upper
temp	time
ultra	beyond, farther, in addition
unda	wave
vacu, vanu	empty
ver	true
vet	old
vi	force
via	way, road
vir, viri	man
vita, viv	life
voci	voice

GREEK-DERIVED ROOTS

Root	Meaning
acme	point, prime

Root	Meaning
acro	topmost, outermost
aer	air
agora	assembly
algo	pain
allo	another, different
ambli	dull
aner, andro	man
ankyl	bent
antho	flower
anthropo	man
apsi	arch
archa	old, ancient
aster, astr	star
atmos	vapor
aura	breeze, breath
auto	self
baro	weight
bary	heavy
basis	step, stand
batho	depth
biblio	book
brachy	short
brady	slow
caco	bad

Root	Meaning
ceno	empty
chari	favor, thanks
chloro	light green
chroa, chroma	color
chrono	time
chryso	gold
cosmo	order, harmony, universe
crato	power
dactyl	finger
de, des	binding
dele	hurt
demo	people
derma	skin, hide
dipl	twofold, doubled
do	giving
doxa, dog	opinion, thought
ecto	outside
endo, ento	within
eon	lifetime
eos	dawn
ergo	work
eros, erot	love
eso	within
ethno	nation

Root	Meaning
etho	custom, character, nature
eury	wide
exo	outside
ge	earth
gen, gene, gon	born, become
geno	race, kind
glossa, glotta	tongue
gramma, graph	letter, something written, small weight
gymno	naked
gyne	woman
gyro	ring, circle
haem	blood
helix	spiral
hetero	other
holo	whole, entire
homalo	even, regular
homo	same
homoi	similar
hora	time, season
horo	boundary
hydro	water
hygro	moist
hypno	sleep

Root	Meaning
ichthy	fish
idea	form, kind
idio	one's own
isos	equal
kine	movement, motion
lepto	small, weak, fine
leuko	white
macro	long
mega	great
mela	black
meso	middle
micro	small
miso	hatred
mne	memory
nema	thread
neo	new
neuro	nerve
nomo	law
oligo	few
onym, onomat	name, noun
ops, opo	eye, face
ortho	straight, right, true
ox, oxy	sharp, acid

Root	Meaning
pachy	thick
pan, pant	all, every
phobo	fear
phone	voice, sound
phos, photo	light
phren	mind
phyle	tribe, race
plat, platy	broad
pneu	breath
pol	city
poly	much, many
psych	breath, life, soul, mind
pyr	fire
schis	split
sema, semato	sign
soma, somato	body
sopho	wise
tachy	swift
tauto	the same
tele	afar, from afar
telo, teleo	end
topo	place
trachy	rugged, tough

ANSWERS TO EXERCISES

EXERCISE 13

pug'	can'did	mit'igate	trium'virate
slant'	al'so	correc'tion	qualifica'tion
fist'	blos'som	beau'tify	ceremo'nial
a'	fra'grant	quan'tity	curios'ity

If you wrote blo'ssom or curio'sity, mark yourself correct.

EXERCISE 16

We've eliminated the author's punctuation marks so that you can more easily see the accent marks:

Life' is re'-al life' is ear'-nest

And' the grave' is not' its goal'

Dust' thou art' to dust' re-turn'-est

Was' not spo'-ken of' the soul'

EXERCISE 18

hundredth, spilled, stows, grandpa, landlubber, gooseberry, fleabitten, yourselves, everything, copycat, fulfill, housemaid, heartfelt, whereupon, hurriedly, accustomed, achieved, accidentally

EXERCISE 20

stopped, dismiss, official, safflower, apron, corrupt, flivver, meddling, tattoo, affix, warrant, digging, until

EXERCISE 21

poking, primary, livelihood, approval, distasteful, arrangement, behavior, chafing, reassurance, protruding, icing, untimely, wiping, introducing, fortunate

EXERCISE 22

changing, carriage, hugely, infringement, imagine, vegetable, raging, staging

EXERCISE 23
naturally, planed, prophesied, wherever, valuable, planned, strictly, undoubtedly, familiar, statement, heroes, hoping, tired, shining, truly, hopping, laid, studying, stopped, skinning, using, becoming, believing, believed, boundaries, buoyant, climbed, decided, desirable, celestial, cement, cigar. The other words come from: certify,

EXERCISE 24
Pigeon, pageant, geography, hygiene, and *surgeon* are not exceptions to the rule because they are not shorter words with added endings. *Pigeon* doesn't come from *pige, pageant* doesn't come from *page, hygiene* doesn't come from *hyge,* and *surgeon* doesn't come from *surge. Gorgeous* and *outrageous* are not exceptions to the rule because the ending *-ous* is excluded from the rule. (*Gorgeous* is a small word plus an ending. The word *gorge* referred to an attractive head-covering worn by women in the middle ages.) *Urgent* follows the rule for adding the ending *-ent* to the word *urge.* The *e* is a helping *e* in *urge,* but part of the ending in *urgent.*

EXERCISE 25
zodiac, rosary, maize, buzzword, exercise, topaz, televising, trapezoidal, eczema, haphazard, zilch

EXERCISE 26
The only words left are cerebral, cerebrum, ceramic, cellestial, cement, cigar. The other words come from: certify, circuit, circle, cease, cent (meaning one hundred), center, century, civil, celebrate, cite, cyclone, cylinder.

EXERCISE 27
sentimental, psychotic, missile, crescent, witless, mistletoe, schism, progressive, classical, anxiousness, oscillate, hustler, nameless, center

EXERCISE 28
Latin-derived: co-, de-, di-, e-, intro-, ne-, prae-, pre-, re-, tre- (ambi-, ante-, bene-, and pene- are always pronounced with short vowel sounds.)

Greek-derived: amphi-, anti-, apo-, auto-, di-, dy-, epi-, eu-, homeo-, homo-, hypo-, ortho-, paleo-, peri-, pro-, tri-. Prefixes ending in *i* and *e* sometimes switch to a short vowel sound, as in the word *predilection.*

EXERCISE 29
nucleus, article, attacked, sacrifice, cavalry, doctor, sincerely, calk, calculate, chlorine, saccharine, synchronize, tobacco, picnicking, rascal, bookkeeping

EXERCISE 30
(1) A silent *u* is inserted. (2) A silent *u* is inserted. The silent *e* is the regular English ending that indicates a long vowel sound before the consonant.

EXERCISE 31
(1) knowledge, partridge, porridge, cartridge; (2) college, privilege; (3) *-age*

EXERCISE 32
carriage, vigilant, vegetable, legitimate, encouraging, agile, agenda, manage

EXERCISE 33
experience, extraordinary, extension, explanation, exorbitant, excellent, toxin, deducts, orthodox, execute

EXERCISE 34
wholly, witch (or which), strength, inkblot, drivel, aqua, acquisitive, critical, ankle

EXERCISE 36
ac-cede, dis-simil-ar, re-edit, sur-rep-titious, in-nate, un-

ne-cess-ary, cor-respond, non-nat-ive, re-en-act, ac-cumulate, co-or-din-ate, pre-ex-ist

EXERCISE 39

resuscitate, collateral, commission, hypocritical, recuperate, impromptu, messenger, inevitable, significance, surprise, tournament

EXERCISE 40

Verbs: appreciate = price, associate = society, depreciate = price, excruciate = crucify, glaciate = glass

Adjectives: (none for ancient), artifice, atrocity, audacity, auspice, avarice, beneficent, capacity, caprice, commerce, (none for crucial or delicious), efficacy, face, fallacy, ferocity, finance, glass, grace, (none for judicial or judicious), loquacity, malice, mendacity, (none for meretricious), office, office, (none for pernicious), perspicacity, price, precocity, prejudice, province, race, rapacity, sacrifice, sagacity, (none for salacious), society, society, space, (none for special, specious, superficial), suspect, tenacity, grace, vice, vivacity, voracity

Nouns: (none for acacia), academic, (none for beautician), clinic, coerce, electric, (none for fiduciary), logic, magic, mathematics, (none for mortician), music, obstetrics, (none for paramecium or patrician), pediatrics, physics, politics, statistics, (none for species), suspect, technical

EXERCISE 41

imaginative, imitation, connection, repetitive, pronunciation, organization, influential, description, inaction, pernicious, dissimilar, adjust, supplemental, suppressing, collateral, commission, immediately

EXERCISE 42

cistern, rhomboid, substantiate, pneumatic, physician, analyze, phenomenon, influential, schedule, cylinder, sincerely

The dictionary tells us that the following words have Latin roots: conception, substantiate, enmity, influential, publicly, sacrifice, sincerely. The rest have Greek roots, except the word *ninth,* which is a native English word, and the word *cistern,* which comes from Old French. (*Criticism* was a Greek word adopted by the Romans.)

EXERCISE 43
arrival, procurement, scheduled, benefited, stretching, reflective, reflexive (notice that *x* is treated as the double-consonant sound it really is), considerate, rebelled, inference, transferring, indemnity, corroding, revelry, confusion, incurred, obliging, corrupted, standardize, conformed, altering, retained, containment

EXERCISE 44
kale, trial, coat, feudal

EXERCISE 45
cleanse (clean), breath (breathe), cleanly (clean), dealt (deal), health (heal), heavy (heave), leapt (leap), meant (mean), pleasant (please), read (read), stealth (steal), treachery (treason), wealthy (weal), zealot (zeal)

EXERCISE 46
Short *e:* bread-bred, breadth-breath, lead-led, read-red, weather-whether; short *i:* been-bin, guild-gild; short *u:* rough-ruff, tough-tuff, done-dun, some-sum, son-sun, won-one

EXERCISE 47
aerial, receive, paid, prairie, copying, lying, hygiene, tragical, weirdness, magically, typifying, fruited, foreign

PLAINFIELD PUBLIC LIBRARY DISTRICT
705 N. Illinois Street
Plainfield, Illinois 60544